Mark Shelton practised in major commercial law firms for thirty years, specialising in property dispute resolution. He has acted for businesses large and small, including FTSE-listed property companies and household-name corporate occupiers, across the whole range of property-related issues.

He is now a full-time commercial property management law trainer, putting his expertise and experience to good use in training both lawyers and surveyors. He delivers training both in-house and for providers including MBL Seminars, Professional Conferences, CPT Events and Solicitors Group. Mark is also the author of a number of books within his areas of expertise.

A Practical Guide to Procedure for Tenants to Terminate Business Tenancies

A Practical Guide to Procedure for Tenants to Terminate Business Tenancies

Mark Shelton
MA (Hons) Law (Cantab), Non-Practising Solicitor
Commercial Property Management Law Trainer
www.marksheltontraining.co.uk

Law Brief Publishing

Published 2021 by Law Brief Publishing, an imprint of Law Brief Publishing Ltd
30 The Parks
Minehead
Somerset
TA24 8BT

www.lawbriefpublishing.com

Paperback: 978-1-913715-96-0

PREFACE

The sole trader or business proprietor who takes a lease of commercial premises will rightly expect the negotiation of the lease to require careful attention. Once it has been signed, and they have taken possession, their focus will naturally shift to the running of the business. They may assume that lease expiry, when it comes around, will be relatively straightforward: the lease has an end date, so it will terminate then, without any further formalities or critical decisions.

While termination of the tenancy can be a straightforward matter, there will often be commercial considerations which require important decisions to be taken first. The business tenant may well be happy to take another lease of the same premises (though that can be dependent on whether some of the terms can be renegotiated). At the same time, an approaching lease expiry is a prompt to look around for other options. Can other premises be found with a better layout, more parking or better transport links, or in a location where there will be more passing trade? If more attractive premises are available, what terms can be negotiated with the landlord?

The tenant will typically want to keep its options open until it has made a firm decision one way or another, and in the case of a tenancy within Part II of the Landlord and Tenant Act 1954, the statutory procedure enables it to do so by prolonging the existing tenancy, potentially for a lengthy period.

If the decision is ultimately to stay put and take a new lease, then the renewal procedure under the 1954 Act will run its course, and the old tenancy will come to end accordingly. This book is not concerned with termination of tenancies in that sense, but with the opposite situation: where the occupier has concluded that it has no further need for the present premises, and intends to vacate them, whether due to relocation or some other reason.

In that case, termination of the tenancy is often a surprisingly technical business. The 1954 Act was enacted for the protection of tenants, but complicates lease termination considerably, since it introduces, on top of any contractual routes to lease termination, a range of statutory procedures, operable at different stages in the life of the lease and in the progress of the procedure under the Act.

The timing of termination is usually an important aspect. The tenant may want it to happen as soon as possible, so as to curtail its rental commitment, or it may have operational reasons for wanting to defer it for a period. Their professional adviser will have to give very careful consideration to what is the appropriate action to achieve termination at the right time. This will be the case whether the client is a sole trader, proprietor of an SME, or a large and sophisticated commercial enterprise.

If the adviser is not an expert on the arcana of the 1954 Act, researching the matter can be time-consuming. The excellent textbooks on the Act are necessarily more wide-ranging and comprehensive, and orderly discussion of the Act as a whole tends to distribute the information which bears on this relatively narrow inquiry across a variety of different sections of the text.

This book, by contrast, is focused on the specific issue. It sets out the available procedures, contractual as well as statutory, starting at day one of the tenancy and progressing through to the expiry date and beyond. As well as exposition of the rules, their application is illustrated in practical scenarios. It is hoped that it will be of use, not only to those practitioners with limited or infrequent exposure to the technicalities of the 1954 Act, but also to the more expert practitioner looking for a quick answer to a very specific problem.

The law is stated as at 27 September 2021.

My thanks are due to Alexander Mulroney of Watson Farley & Williams LLP for some thought-provoking exchanges, which I have gratefully drawn upon for the purposes of this book.

Mark Shelton
September 2021

CONTENTS

CHAPTER ONE

OVERVIEW OF SECURITY OF TENURE FOR BUSINESSES

This chapter provides an overview of the scheme of business security of tenure under Part II of the Landlord and Tenant Act 1954.

For the reader who has not yet acquired familiarity with it, or who would welcome a reminder, a précis of Part II of the 1954 Act will be helpful. Although what follows is an overview, there is no avoiding the highly technical nature of the Act; its scheme is complicated and ingenious, and works well, though one may wish that it could operate with greater simplicity.

Background

Twenty years or more ago, on Tottenham Court Road in central London, just north of the junction with Oxford Street, there used to stand a number of rather ramshackle single-storey buildings forming a short row of shops, mostly selling hi-fi and other electrical goods. Their scruffy and mixed appearance, and low height, was rather at odds with the generally high quality of the immediately surrounding buildings, many of them recently developed, mixed-use developments over multiple storeys. Looking over the site from the vantage point of any of those higher buildings, one could see that behind the row of shops was an unused, overgrown, brownfield site.

This was reportedly the last remaining bombsite left over from World War II in central London, and now it too has been developed. The shops at street level form part of a smart, modern building, and some of the occupiers of the former row of shops have evidently taken leases there. It is entirely likely that they found themselves in a position to do so thanks to the operation of *Part II* of the *Landlord and Tenant Act 1954*, which is fitting if so, since it was bomb damage which led to the enactment of that legislation in the first place.

The bombing of London, Coventry, Liverpool, Plymouth and other cities during World War II resulted, of course, in widespread, major damage. As regards commercial property, many offices, shops, factories, workshops, warehouses and other premises were destroyed. By a simple application of the law of supply and demand, the rental value of remaining commercial property was increased, and landlords were in a dominant negotiating position. Tenants unable to afford higher rents would be obliged to vacate their premises when the lease came to an end, and some would thereby lose significant goodwill built up by decades of trading at those premises. To afford protection to business tenants, therefore, Parliament enacted *Part II* of the *Landlord and Tenant Act 1954*, conferring security of tenure on them.

As described above, there is now no remaining World War II bomb damage in Central London, and there must be very little elsewhere in the United Kingdom. There is a more than respectable argument for repeal: no other jurisdiction in the world has a similar system; it is an interference with the free market and with landowners' property rights; and the original justification for its creation has disappeared. At the time of writing, part of the government's response to the Covid-19 pandemic has been to announce a wide-ranging review of commercial property law, expressly including the role of the 1954 Act.

However, the Act has been around for 67 years now, it is very familiar to landlords and tenants, and its impact is 'priced in'. Government may well conclude that it continues to provide useful protection to business tenants, and should be retained.

Legislation and amendments

There are quite a number of Landlord and Tenant Acts, but there is only one, the 1954 Act, which is regularly referred to as "*the* Landlord and Tenant Act". It is also colloquially called "the 1954 Act", and sometimes even just "the Act", such is its central importance to commercial landlord and tenant law. To be accurate, it is Part II of the 1954 Act with which we are concerned (Part I deals with certain long residential leases), but it will generally be more convenient throughout to use the designation 'the

1954 Act' or 'the Act' rather than '*Part II* of the *Landlord and Tenant Act 1954*'.

The Act has been subject to a number of amendments, as might be expected over a 67-year period. Most significantly:

a) The *Law of Property Act 1969* introduced the ability to contract out of the Act, also the availability of interim rent; and

b) The *Regulatory Reform (Business Tenancies) (England and Wales) Order 2003 (SI 2003/3096)* enacted a wide-ranging raft of reforms to the Act, following a lengthy consultation exercise.

To understand the operation of the Act in its current form, it will sometimes be necessary to refer back to how it stood prior to certain of those amendments.

Core principles

There are three principles which form the heart of the 1954 Act.

- When the date is reached upon which a tenancy within the Act should (contractually speaking) terminate, it does not do so. Instead, it continues under *s.24(1)*, and is sometimes then referred to as the 'continuation tenancy'. This state of affairs continues indefinitely, until such time as action is taken by either landlord or tenant to terminate the tenancy in accordance with the Act.

- When such action is taken, the tenant will generally be entitled to a new lease, and should therefore not have to vacate the premises. Further protection is given to the tenant by provision in the Act which regulates the content of the new lease (*ss.32-35*), most importantly the rent. The procedure under the Act is therefore referred to as 'lease renewal', and the new lease granted as a result may be called the 'renewal lease'.

- The landlord is not thereby deprived of its property indefinitely, since it has the right to oppose the grant of a new tenancy on specified statutory grounds. Any 'ground of opposition' on which the landlord relies must be proven in court; if it is, the tenancy terminates, and no new tenancy is granted. Unless the ground of opposition which ultimately leads to the refusal of a new tenancy includes some element of responsibility on the tenant's part (e.g. persistent delay in paying rent), the landlord will be required to pay compensation to the tenant upon termination, calculated as provided for in the Act.

s.23(1) – Cornerstone of the Act

The first provision of Part II of the Act is *s.23*, and it lays down the qualifications for protection:

> *(1) Subject to the provisions of this Act, this Part of this Act applies to any tenancy where the property comprised in the tenancy is or includes premises which are occupied by the tenant and are so occupied for the purposes of a business carried on by him or for those and other purposes.*

There are thus three elements to protection:

- a tenancy;

- a business; and

- occupation.

Each requires further comment.

Tenancy

'Tenancy' is defined in *s.69(1)*, and includes both tenancies and sub-tenancies. It also includes agreements for lease (or sub-lease). It does not include licences to occupy or tenancies at will. Periodic tenancies fall within the Act, and receive special treatment in some ways, which will be considered later.

The definition of tenancy in *s.69(1)* does not exclude sub-tenancies granted out of tenancies which do not have the protection of the Act, so a tenant whose lease is contracted-out may nevertheless grant a sub-tenancy which falls within the Act.

Also, a sub-lease granted in breach of an alienation restriction in the headlease will nevertheless have security of tenure: *D'Silva v Lister House Developments Ltd [1971] Ch 17.*

Business

"Business" is defined as a trade, profession or employment, and includes any activity carried on by a body of persons whether corporate or incorporate (*s.23(2)*). There are thus different tests for an individual tenant and a body of persons, though nothing seems to turn on this in practice. Further guidance is to be had from caselaw, which shows that 'business' includes activities such as sports clubs, local government offices and schools. Broadly, anything that is not residential is likely to be considered 'business', although *s.43(1)* expressly excludes tenancies within the agricultural tenancies legislation, and mining leases, while leases of telecoms sites are excluded by *s.43(4)*.

The cases show an area of uncertainty in relation to occupation for charitable and community purposes. In *Secretary of State for Transport v Jenkins (2000) 79 P&CR 118*, for example, use as a community free farm was held not to constitute a business. Although there need not be any goal of making a profit, there does have to be some activity of a commercial nature, and activity carried out only for 'public benevolence' will not qualify.

However, the definition has generally been construed widely. The only significant area of difficulty relates to businesses whose main activity is sub-letting, which raises questions about the extent to which the tenant is in occupation. This will be considered in relation to the concept of occupation.

Under *s.23(4)*, the tenancy will fall within the Act even where use for the specific type of business carried on there is prohibited by the lease. If, for example, the lease provides that the premises are only to be used for the sale of footwear, but in fact they are used for the sale of ironmongery, the tenant will still enjoy security of tenure. If, however, the lease prohibits *any* business use, then neither sale of footwear or ironmongery, nor any other commercial use, would bring the tenancy within the Act.

Where the occupier is not the tenant

The wording of *s.23(1)* effectively requires that the business occupier and the tenant should be one and the same. This has potential to cause problems in common commercial situations. For example, while a small business may have been incorporated, a landlord may prefer to grant a lease to the proprietor of the business personally, either because the company may not be able to show a sufficient trading record, or because the landlord simply prefers that the business proprietor should be liable to enforcement against personal assets in the event of default on the lease covenants. In that case, since it would be the company in business occupation of the premises, the proprietor, as tenant, would not qualify for security of tenure under *s.23*.

This and related issues were among the matters addressed when the Act was reformed in 2003, and the general principle now is that an individual and the company that they control are treated as one and the same for the purposes of the operation of the Act: *ss.23(1A), 23(1B), 30(1A), 30(1B)*.

In the same way, where a lease is held by a company, business occupation by another company within the same group of companies is treated as business occupation by the tenant (*s.42*). There is also specific provision to overcome this potential difficulty in relation to premises held on trust (*s.41*) and partnership premises (*s.41A*).

Mixed-use premises

It is apparent from the wording of *s.23* that the Act applies where only part of the premises is occupied for business purposes. That might be the case, for instance, in the very commonly encountered letting arrangement of a shop with a flat above it, all let together on one lease. In such a case, the obvious question is whether the tenancy is protected under the 1954 Act as a business tenancy, or under the *Rent Act 1977* or the *Housing Act 1988* as a residential tenancy.

This is a question with real practical significance, because of the different degrees of protection afforded to tenants by the different statutory regimes. Under the 1954 Act, as we have said, the landlord may obtain possession at the end of the tenancy if it can prove one of the statutory grounds of opposition. Protection under the *Rent Act 1977* is much stronger, and may be transmitted to family members upon the death of the tenant, so that recovery of possession may be practically impossible for decades. Recovery of possession under the *Housing Act 1988* has been quite straightforward, though a gradual accretion of protections and restrictions has increased the difficulties for landlords over recent years.

The qualifying condition for residential protection is that the property must be "*let as a separate dwelling*". This wording has a long pedigree in the residential legislation, going back as far as 1915. Note that if premises are *let* as a dwelling, but *occupied* partly or wholly for business purposes, on the face of it both schemes of protection would apply.

That outcome is prevented by *s.24(3), Rent Act 1977*, and also *s.1(2)* and *para 4* of *Sched 1, Housing Act 1988*, both of which specifically provide that the respective Acts cannot apply to a tenancy which falls within Part II of the 1954 Act. In effect, the business security of tenure regime 'trumps' the residential.

There is a limitation, in this context, to the meaning of 'business occupation'. If the business use is so limited that it is regarded as incidental to the residential occupation, then the 1954 Act will not apply. For example, in *Gurton v Parrott [1991] EGLR 98* a lady had occupied a property since 1939 as her home, although she was only granted a tenancy of it in 1974. At that time, and for some years afterwards, various outbuildings and land comprised within the property were used for her business of dog-kennelling, grooming and breeding, and the landlord subsequently gave notice to terminate under the 1954 Act, asserting that she had a business tenancy. The court held that she occupied the property as her residence, and that the running of the business there was incidental to that: "*something akin to a hobby*". That meant that her tenancy was protected under one of the predecessors to the *Rent Act 1977*, and she was effectively irremoveable. This 'incidental use' exception has never applied in any recorded case since, and seems to be very limited.

There are some dicta in decided cases (e.g. *Broadway Investments Hackney Ltd v Grant [2006] EWCA Civ 1709*), to suggest that a lease might move out of residential protection into business protection, or vice versa. In *Tan v Sitkowski [2007] EWCA Civ 30*, Neuberger LJ had no difficulty with the idea that a tenant might have been granted a residential tenancy under the Rent Act, then use the premises wholly or partly for business purposes, thus coming within the ambit of the 1954 Act, and subsequently cease the business use and return to the fold of the Rent Act. There does not appear, though, to be any case in which a court has actually decided that this has happened. It would in any event depend on the tenancy not prohibiting business use; if there were such a prohibition, the 1954 Act could not apply (*s.23(4)*), and the lease would remain within the Rent Act throughout.

A more common situation might be that premises are originally let for mixed business and residential use, within the 1954 Act, as will usually be the case in relation to a shop-and-flat lease, but the tenant gives up the business while continuing to live there. If there is no longer any business use, the tenancy will have ceased to be a business tenancy within the 1954 Act, so does the tenant thereby gain the protection of the 1977 or 1988 Act? That was the issue in *Tan v Sitkowski*, where it was held that residential protection had not been acquired, as it could not be said that the premises had been "*let as a separate dwelling*".

It may be noted, finally, that *s.35* of the *Small Business, Enterprise and Employment Act 2015* inserted a new section, *s.43ZA*, into the 1954 Act, to prevent 'accidental' business security of tenure being acquired where people run businesses from their rented homes.

It applies where:

- Property is let as a dwelling

- The tenancy specifies residential use, but also permits the tenant to run a business from home

- The tenant carries on a business of a nature *"which might reasonably be carried on at home"*.

In those circumstances the tenant will not have security of tenure.

Occupation

To come within *s.23(1)*, it is not enough that the premises should be let for the purposes of a business, they must also be occupied for that purpose. Occupation is an important qualification for protection under the 1954 Act, and indeed under *s.27(1A)* of the Act the statutory continuation tenancy will not arise if at the expiry of the lease the tenant has gone out of occupation. Occupation can be relevant to other matters, as well as the basic question of whether a tenancy falls within the Act, such as the rate of compensation payable to a tenant where a landlord successfully opposes the renewal of a lease.

Occupation may still qualify if it is for uses which are purely ancillary to the business, as in *Hancock & Willis v GMS Syndicate (1983) 265 EG 473*, in which solicitors used certain premises purely for storing files and occasional business lunches. That still qualified as occupation for the purposes of their business. A more common example might be the arrangement found in many shopping centres, where the tenant has a lease of its shop, and a separate lease of a storage unit elsewhere in the centre. As regards the storage unit, it is not being used for retailing, which is the tenant's core business activity, but storage is ancillary to the business, so the occupation will attract security of tenure.

Where the tenant's business is sub-letting the premises, then it becomes problematic to regard them as remaining in occupation, though depending on the specific factual circumstances they may have retained sufficient control of the premises to qualify for protection under the Act.

In *Lee Verhulst (Investments) Ltd v Harwood Trust [1973] QB 204*, the tenant carried on the business of letting furnished service rooms, and was nevertheless held to occupy the whole premises for the purposes of a business. The important factor was that the tenant exercised an unusually high degree of control over the sub-let parts, and provided services for the sub-tenants.

The important factors to consider in such situations, the court held, are:

- Has the tenant sub-let the whole of the premises?

- Does the tenant supply any services to the sub-let parts?

- Does the tenant devote time and resources to the management of the sub-let parts?

- Does the tenant exercise a high degree of control over the sub-let parts?

The *Lee Verhulst* case must now be read in the light of the House of Lords decision in *Graysim Holdings Ltd v P&O Property Holdings Ltd [1996] AC 329*. The case concerned a market, held on a lease. Much of the space was sub-let to stall-holders. As a matter of principle (perhaps also as a matter of physics), premises cannot be occupied for business purposes by two occupiers simultaneously, as then both would be entitled to renew their leases under the 1954 Act. But whether it is the sub-tenant stall-holder or the head-tenant which can be said to be in occupation is a question of fact and degree.

On the facts, the stall-holders enjoyed exclusive possession of their stalls, and had business tenancies. While the head-tenant retained some common parts and provided services, that could not be said to be occupation for the purposes of a business. The reason for that was that the stall-holders would, under the structure of the 1954 Act, renew their sub-leases direct with the superior landlord, and once all of the stall sub-leases had become head-leases in this way, the head-tenant's business would no longer exist.

It seems to follow that it will be more difficult for a head-landlord to establish that it is in business occupation where the sub-lettings are of a commercial nature.

A question which often arises is whether a tenant is in occupation despite not having a physical presence at the premises for a time (for example, having moved out because of fire damage). The courts have dealt with this by developing the concept of the 'thread of continuity of business occupation', and asking whether in any particular set of circumstances it has been broken.

In *I & H Caplan Ltd v Caplan & Anor [1963] 2 All ER 930*, the question was whether the tenant had lost the protection of the Act by going out of occupation. Prompted by the landlord's initial success (later overturned on appeal) in opposing the grant of a new lease, the tenant had ceased trading for over six months, and relocated stock to other premises. However, the tenant intended to resume trading if the application for a new tenancy was successful, and did resume trading after success in the appeal hearing. It was held that the tenant had not lost protection simply by ceasing physically to occupy. This was a borderline case, but the thread of continuity was not broken.

Morrison Holdings Ltd v Manders Property (Wolverhampton) Ltd [1976] 1 EGLR 70 also concerned whether the tenant had lost security of tenure. There, the premises were badly damaged by fire, entitling the landlord under the terms of the lease to give notice terminating the tenancy forthwith. About a month later, the landlord demolished what was left of the premises. The court held that the tenant had not abandoned occupation, but intended to go back as soon as the premises were fit for occupation, and had not therefore lost protection.

Bacchiocchi v Academic Agency Ltd [1998] 3 EGLR 157 is perhaps the most extreme example, and concerned the question whether the tenant was entitled to compensation where the landlord had successfully opposed the grant of a new tenancy. That in turn depended on whether the tenant had been in occupation for the five years immediately preceding the end of the tenancy. In fact, having been in occupation for twenty years, the tenant vacated the premises twelve days before the lease terminated. The court considered that where premises are empty for a short period, whether at the beginning or end of the term, or mid-term, that is a 'normal incident of business occupation', and does not break the continuity of occupation. The tenant should not have to resort to devices like storage of goods or token visits in order to maintain that it was in occupation. The tenant was entitled to compensation.

Overview of procedure

The Act preserves, by virtue of *s.24(2)*, certain common law methods of lease termination: forfeiture, surrender, and notice to quit given by the tenant. If a lease is terminated by any of those methods, there is no right to renew, and no need for the procedure now described to be followed.

s.25 notice or s.26 request

Either the landlord or the tenant may initiate the lease renewal process. The landlord can do so by serving on the tenant a notice under *s.25*, or the tenant can do so by serving on the landlord a different type of notice, referred to as a 'request for a new tenancy', under *s.26*. There can be only one effective notice, however: if the landlord has served a *s.25* notice, the tenant cannot validly serve a *s.26* request, and vice versa (*s.26(4)*).

A *s.25* notice terminates the existing tenancy, and must specify a termination date. A *s.26* request must specify a commencement date for the requested new tenancy, but the effect is also to define the termination date for the existing tenancy, on the date immediately before the specified commencement date (*s.26(5)*). Thus, the effect of either type of notice is to terminate the existing tenancy, or continuation tenancy which arises under *s.24(1)*, on the specified date.

The date specified in the notice, whether under *s.25* or *s.26*, must be from six to twelve months after service of the notice, and cannot be earlier than the contractual expiry date. Therefore, notice cannot be given earlier than the date which is twelve months before the contractual expiry. In the last twelve months of the term, the length of notice cannot, initially, be any less than the remaining time up to the contractual expiry date, but once that remaining time reduces to less than six months, or once the contractual expiry date has passed, the length of notice can be anything from six to twelve months. These time limits are absolutely strict, and the Act contains no provision for them to be varied by the parties.

Landlord's ground of opposition

At this early stage, the landlord must specify whether or not it intends to oppose the grant of a new tenancy, and if so on what grounds. If the process is commenced by a *s.25* notice, the ground of opposition must have been set out in that notice. If it is a *s.26* request which initiated matters, the landlord has two months in which it may (but is not obliged to) serve a counternotice under *s.26(6)*, indicating whether it will oppose the grant of a new tenancy, and if so on what ground. The landlord will not subsequently be able to rely in court upon any ground of opposition which has not been specified at this point (*s.30(1)*).

The landlord therefore has to consider carefully whether, and if so on what basis, it intends to oppose renewal. The decision has irrevocable consequences, since what the landlord does in this regard may affect whether any compensation is payable to the tenant, and if so how much. If the landlord's notice or counternotice specifies a ground of opposition which entitles the tenant to compensation, that entitlement cannot be cancelled by the landlord withdrawing the ground of opposition. Once the ground has been specified in this way, the tenant may at any time abandon the renewal process, vacate the premises, and claim the compensation.

Court application

Should the landlord decide to oppose renewal, its ground of opposition will have to be proved in court, if the tenant resists termination of the tenancy. If the renewal is unopposed, however, it may still be necessary for there to be a hearing, since it is for the court to decide upon the terms of the new tenancy, if the parties are unable to agree them.

The scheme of the Act envisages the court application being made at a relatively early stage in the process. Application may be made following service of either a *s.25* notice or a *s.26* request (in the latter case, either a *s.26(6)* counternotice must have been served by the landlord, or the time for doing so must have expired). The latest date at which an application can be made is the termination/commencement date set out in the *s.25* notice/*s.26* request. It follows that the deadline is from six to twelve months after service of the initial notice, depending upon what date was specified in it.

The parties can agree to extend this deadline, under *s.29B*, inserted into the Act as part of the 2003 reforms. Successive agreed extensions are commonplace, and many lease renewals are resolved without involving the courts at all.

If no application to the court is made before the expiry of the time limit, or of any current extension of the time limit, the old tenancy will come to an end on the date specified in the *s.25* notice or *s.26* request, and the tenant will have to vacate. This is, for the tenant, one of the most important deadlines in the Act, and strict diary discipline is required to ensure it is not missed, since a negligence claim will inevitably follow if it is. The ability to agree to extend the time may appear to make this less crucial, but if, say, three successive extensions of the original deadline are agreed, that represents four opportunities to get things wrong, instead of just one, so diary discipline is as important as it ever was.

There are potentially three different types of court application:

- The tenant may make an application for an order for the grant of a new tenancy, under *s.24(1)*.

- Equally, the landlord may make an application for an order for the grant of a new tenancy, also under *s.24(1)*.

- A landlord who opposes renewal may take the initiative by making an application under *s.29(2)*, for the termination of the tenancy without any new tenancy being granted.

As there can be only one effective initiating notice, so there can be only one effective court application. If the tenant has made a *s.24(1)* application, then the landlord can make no application under either s.24(1) or s.29(2), by virtue of s.24(2A) and s.29(3). On the other hand, if the landlord has got in first with an application of either sort, then the tenant may not make an application under s.24(1) (see s.24(2A) and (2B)).

Continuation of tenancy pending outcome of court proceedings

Whichever is the effective type of application, and whichever party is the claimant, once it has been made then the existing tenancy will be further continued by the operation of s.64, up until three months after final disposal of the court proceedings.

This potentially presents an opportunity for the landlord to make the court application and then withdraw it, so terminating the tenancy without the necessity to prove a ground of opposition or pay compensation. That eventuality was anticipated, and provided for in s.24(2C) and s.29(6), which prevent withdrawal of a landlord's application without the consent of the tenant.

During the continuation period, all terms of the existing tenancy still apply, though it is open to either party to have an 'interim rent' determined, so that the rental level during the continuation period can be adjusted.

Court order

If a s.24(1) application is made, s.29(1) requires the court to make an order for the grant of a new tenancy, subject to the other provisions of Part II. However, if the landlord establishes one of the seven grounds of opposition set out in s.30(1), the court shall not make an order for the grant of a new tenancy, but shall make an order for the termination of the tenancy without any new tenancy being granted; if not, there will be an order for the grant of a new tenancy (s.29(4) and s.31(1)).

Summary

Business tenancies within the 1954 Act do not come to an end on their contractual expiry date, but continue indefinitely, unless and until terminated in accordance with the Act. When terminated, the tenant is entitled to a new tenancy, on regulated terms, although the landlord may oppose renewal on seven statutory grounds. Depending on which ground is relied upon, a landlord who succeeds in resisting the grant of a new tenancy may have to pay the tenant compensation.

The Act applies to tenancies and sub-tenancies, whether fixed-term or periodic, but not to tenancies at will or licences to occupy. There must be occupation of at least part of the premises for business purposes, and 'business' is given a wide interpretation by the courts.

The renewal process is initiated by either a s.25 notice served by the landlord, or a s.26 request served by the tenant, and strict time limits apply to the timing of service and length of notice. The landlord must, at this initial stage, identify whether it intends to oppose the renewal, and if so on what ground, thus potentially incurring liability to pay compensation.

The next procedural step is an application to court, which must be made by either landlord or tenant. The deadline for doing that is the date specified in the s.25 notice or s.26 request, though the parties can agree to extend it. If no court application is made in time, the tenancy comes to an end at the deadline, and the tenant loses security of tenure and must vacate.

Once a court application has been made, the tenancy continues until three months after the court proceedings have been finally determined.

CHAPTER TWO

TERMINATION BY TENANT'S CONTRACTUAL NOTICE

This chapter considers termination of tenancies by means of contractual notice, which may be done outside the procedural structures of the 1954 Act. It deals with both periodic tenancies, and exercise of break options.

We noted in Chapter 1 that under *s.24(2)* of the 1954 Act, certain common law methods of lease termination are preserved: forfeiture, surrender, and notice to quit given by the tenant. If a lease is terminated by any of those methods, there is no right to renew, and no need to serve any notices under the Act. In this chapter we consider the third of those methods: notice to quit given by the tenant.

Notice to quit under a periodic tenancy

Nature of periodic tenancy

A periodic tenancy is a recurring arrangement. Typically, the recurrence is weekly, monthly, quarterly or annual. If, for example, a periodic tenancy is granted on a yearly basis, then strictly speaking the tenant has a tenancy for a year; when it comes to an end a new tenancy for a further year automatically arises, and when that comes to an end another new tenancy for a further year automatically arises, and so on and so on indefinitely, until the arrangement is terminated by one or other party serving a notice to terminate.

Periodic tenancies and the 1954 Act

Periodic tenancies receive distinctive treatment under the 1954 Act.

a) Because service by the tenant of a notice to quit is one of the common law methods of lease termination which is preserved by *s.24(2)*, the statutory continuation tenancy under *s.24(1)* will not arise upon expiry of the tenant's notice.

b) As a matter of contract, either landlord or tenant can serve notice to terminate a periodic tenancy. A landlord may wish to do so in order to obtain an updated open market rent. However, a periodic tenancy is necessarily within the Act (see point (d)), so that a common law notice to quit, served by the landlord, will not by itself terminate the tenancy. The landlord would also have to serve a notice in accordance with *s.25* (in practice this may often serve as the common law notice to quit as well), upon which the tenant would be entitled to apply for a new tenancy.

It is not necessary, though, to require a tenant to go through the hoops of the 1954 Act. If they are content for the tenancy to continue, then they can simply do nothing; their position is in this respect the same as a fixed-term tenant with the protection of the Act. If, though, they wish it to come to an end, then they do not need the protection conferred by the Act. It is for this reason that a *s.26* request can only be served in relation to "*a tenancy for a term of years certain*", and not in relation to a periodic tenancy.

This inability to initiate the renewal process does mean that if a business tenant holding under a periodic tenancy finds that the rental market has fallen and it is paying over the odds for its premises, it cannot secure a renewed tenancy with rent determined at the open market level. All it can do is give contractual notice to terminate the tenancy, and look for other premises.

c) A misconception sometimes arises in relation to the operation of *s.43(3)*, which provides that tenancies for six months or less fall outside the Act. There is an exception to this rule in favour of tenants who have accrued twelve months' continuous business occupation, who therefore have security of tenure even if occupying under a tenancy for six months or less. It is sometimes mistakenly thought, because of this, that a periodic tenant has no security of tenure unless and until they have been in occupation for twelve months. That is to misread *s.43(3)*, which also applies only to tenancies *"for a term certain"*. The true position is that a periodic tenant has security of tenure from the moment they go into business occupation.

d) The ability to contract out a new lease also only applies to tenancies *"for a term of years certain"* (*s.38A*), so a periodic tenancy cannot be contracted-out. It follows that a periodic tenant in business occupation must always have security of tenure under the Act.

Creation of periodic tenancies

Periodic tenancies may be created by express agreement. They fall under *s.54(2)* of the *Law of Property Act 1925*, and therefore do not need to be created by deed. They may be created by a simple contract under hand, or even by an oral agreement. They may also arise by implication, in circumstances where the parties have made no agreement, even an oral one, as to the basis of occupation. Typically, this might be where a tenant is allowed into occupation in advance of a lease being executed, or where a tenant holds over, paying rent, after termination of a contracted-out lease.

If, however, the parties are negotiating for a new tenancy, a court would be likely to find instead an implied tenancy at will: *Javad v Aqil [1991] 1 WLR 1007*. The decision in *Erimus Housing Limited v Barclays Wealth Trustees (Jersey) Limited [2014] EWCA Civ 303* confirmed that approach. The landlord in that case argued that negotiations had petered out, and that the arrangement had 'hardened' into a periodic tenancy (the practical result of that being, on the facts of the case, that the tenant would be liable for almost a whole year's rent). The Court of Appeal disagreed; even though negotiations had been 'desultory' and 'sporadic', the occupation had begun against the background of negotiations for a new lease, and nothing had happened to change that.

Where a periodic tenancy is implied, it will be necessary to identify the period of recurrence: is it quarterly, yearly, monthly, etc.? It might be natural to assume that if the rent is paid quarterly then it is a quarterly tenancy, but the courts' approach is to look instead at the basis on which the rent is calculated. If the rent is expressed in annual terms, as is almost invariably the case, then it is highly likely to be considered an annual periodic tenancy (*Prudential Assurance Co Ltd v London Residuary Body [1992] 3 All ER 504 (HL)*).

Most commercial periodic tenancies are annual in nature, in fact, since not only implied tenancies, but also express periodic tenancies of commercial premises tend to be annual.

Length of notice to quit

An express, written periodic tenancy agreement will almost always specify the required length of notice to terminate. The parties may not have considered this in the case of a purely oral agreement, and in any event the evidence as to what was agreed orally might be scant. As regards an implied periodic tenancy, or an express one, written or oral, in which provision as to length of notice is lacking or cannot be established, the court applies a common law rule to determine the required notice period.

The common law rule is that the landlord must give at least one full period's notice, expiring on the final day of a period. In the case of an annual periodic tenancy, though, the minimum period is six months, not one year (*Prudential Assurance Co Ltd v London Residuary Body [1992] 3 All ER 504 (HL)*). Since most commercial periodic tenancies, express or implied, are annual ones, this is the usual position. Hence, if a client gives instructions on 1 November to terminate a periodic tenancy which runs annually from 1 October, a six-month notice would not be valid as it would not expire on the final day of the annual period. The earliest expiry date which could be specified in a notice to quit would be the following 1 October, eleven months away.

Determining the final day of the period may be difficult in the case of an implied or oral tenancy, and may necessitate the service of multiple notices providing for different likely dates.

An express written agreement may well provide for notice to be given in writing, may provide for methods of service, and should contain an address for the landlord, at which notices may be served. In the absence of helpful provisions of this nature, and especially in the case of an implied tenancy, it may be necessary to serve notice by multiple methods, and perhaps at multiple addresses, to be sure of effecting service.

Where there are joint tenants holding under a periodic tenancy, notice to quit given by one of them will be effective to terminate the tenancy (*Hammersmith and Fulham LBC v Monk [1992] 1 AC 478*).

Further consideration is given to the practicalities of drafting and serving notices in Chapter 4.

Exercise of break option

Use of break options

Break options are increasingly prevalent in commercial occupancy arrangements of all kinds. As the average term length of new leases has declined over recent decades, a familiar feature of lease negotiations has been tenants seeking a shorter term than landlords would wish them to take. An obvious way to resolve that is to grant a lease of the length that the landlord prefers, but incorporating a break option in the tenant's favour.

The pre-existing trend towards shorter lease terms and more break options has been intensified and accelerated by the economic uncertainty created in recent years by a combination of Brexit and Covid-19. Occupiers in most sectors now prioritise flexibility in their occupational arrangements. Associated with this, in the retail sector, has been a renewed interest in turnover-based rents, and leases incorporating such a mechanism for calculating the rent will very often contain break options, so that the landlord can terminate the lease if the tenant fails to achieve the expected turnover. Break options in turnover leases are usually mutual.

The upshot of all this is that many more leases than in former years now contain tenant's break options, even leases granted for a short term. A five-year lease with a break at year three, for example, would be by no means unusual.

Break options and the 1954 Act

A tenant's break notice is regarded as the same as a tenant's notice to quit for the purpose of *s.24(2)*, and so has the effect of terminating the tenancy with no right to renew, and no further required action under the 1954 Act. This was much debated for a period, in relation to the question whether, in a falling rental market, a tenant might serve a break notice, followed by a *s.26* request, so as to obtain a new lease at a reduced rent. The issue came before the court in *Garston v Scottish Widows Fund and Life Assurance Society [1998] 1 WLR 1583*, where the tenant had followed precisely that course, and the court held that the *s.26* request was ineffective.

Of course, service of a break notice by a landlord does not fall within *s.24(2)*. For a landlord's break to be effective, either the tenancy must be contracted-out, or the landlord must serve a *s.25* notice as well, and oppose the grant of a new lease. *Receiver for the Metropolitan Police District v Palacegate Properties Ltd [2000] EWCA Civ 33* confirmed that a lease containing a break option is a *"tenancy for a term of years certain"* within the meaning of *s.38A*, and can therefore be validly contracted out.

Challenges to exercise of break options

In difficult economic circumstances when the rental market is falling, tenants will be more inclined to exercise break options, while landlords are likely to resist the operation of the break if they can. This has given rise to a great deal of caselaw.

Exercise of a break can present difficulties: first as regards compliance with the formalities of service; and secondly because various conditions commonly need to be satisfied if the break is to be valid. In this chapter we focus on conditionality, while Chapter 4 covers formalities of serving notices generally.

The *RICS Professional Statement: Code for Leasing Business Premises* ("the *Lease Code*") provides that break options should be conditional only on

a) there being no arrears of principal rent (i.e. not including items such as service charge and insurance premiums, even if expressed to be rent), and

b) the tenant giving up occupation, and leaving no sub-tenants or other occupiers.

It further provides that disputes about the state of the premises, or what has been left behind or removed, should be settled later, as at normal lease expiry.

Condition for payment of rent

Where the break is conditional, the conditions will invariably include payment of rent up to date. Unless the break date happens to be the final day of the quarter (or other rental period), the question arises whether the final advance instalment of rent falls to be apportioned. If, for example, rent is payable in advance on the usual quarter days, and the break date is 10 October, must the tenant pay a full quarter's rent on the immediately preceding 29 September, or is it entitled to pay a lesser amount, pro-rated to reflect the 12 days' possession which it will have?

It was argued by the tenant in *Capital & City Holdings Ltd v Dean Warburg [1989] 1 EGLR 90* (a case concerning termination by forfeiture, not break notice) that the usual general wording in the *reddendum* clause, identifying the rent as *"£[x] per annum or a proportionate part in respect of any period of less than a year"* required an apportionment where the tenancy was brought to an end in mid-quarter. The court rejected this argument, and while the decision may perhaps have been coloured by the context of forfeiture, the conclusion on this point has been followed in a sufficient number of cases to be regarded as absolutely settled.

It follows that there will be no apportionment unless there is clear, specific wording. This type of provision is now more common in leases, and indeed the *Lease Code* provides that leases should require landlords to repay any rent, service charge or insurance paid by the tenant for any period after a break takes effect.

There was an attempt, in *Marks and Spencer Plc v BNP Paribas Securities Services Trust Company (Jersey) Ltd [2015] UKSC 72*, to establish an entitlement to an apportionment in the absence of any such specific express provision. The argument relied upon an implied term to the effect that once the break had operated, the tenant was entitled to be refunded the 'overpayment'. However, both the Court of Appeal and the Supreme Court held that the test for implication of a term set out in *Attorney General of Belize and others v Belize Telecom Ltd [2009] UKPC 10* was not satisfied.

It follows that, unless there is specific provision for apportionment, the tenant must pay the whole quarter's rent. Despite this unpromising legal background, it is often possible to persuade the landlord to refund the 'overpayment' later. Also, lease termination is routinely accompanied by a dilapidations claim, and an unapportioned final rental payment may serve to reduce or eliminate the 'loss of rent' element in the calculation of the damages payable to the landlord.

Condition that all payments are up to date

Where there is a condition that all payments due under the lease must be up to date, the standard of compliance required is strict: every penny must be paid. In *Avocet Industrial Estates LLP v Merol Ltd [2011] EWHC 3422 (Ch)*, for example, failure to satisfy a condition of this nature invalidated the attempted exercise of the break where the sum involved was only some £150. The outstanding sum was interest due on a historic late payment of rent, which had never been calculated or demanded prior to the break date, but which was nevertheless held to be due.

It can be difficult to be sure that absolutely everything which was ever due under the lease has been paid, particularly where the tenant has been in occupation for several years. Tenants will sometimes pay an extra amount to be on the safe side, and then reclaim it once the break has successfully operated.

Landlords may raise demands at the last minute, for insurance premiums, balancing service charge payments, interest, or other sums. Tenants who anticipate this may want to make sure that their solicitors are in funds, and sufficiently authorised, to pay any such amounts.

The lease will usually prohibit any deductions or set-off in relation to payments due under the lease, so tenants should avoid, for example, trying to recoup rent deposit monies in this way. Any such sum should be claimed later. Equally, if any sums are disputed, the tenant should pay on a without prejudice basis, and reclaim them later.

Condition for vacant possession

A condition that the tenant should give vacant possession is common. 'Vacant possession' was defined in *NYK Logistics (UK) Limited v Ibrend Estates BV [2011] EWCA Civ 683* as meaning that:

> "...*the property is empty of people and that the purchaser is able to assume and enjoy immediate and exclusive possession, occupation and control of it. It must also be empty of chattels, although the obligation in this respect is likely only to be breached if any chattels left in the property substantially prevent or interfere with the enjoyment of the right of possession of a substantial part of the property.*"

Tenant's fixtures, as well as chattels, sometimes cause a problem in this regard. These might include, for example, suspended ceilings, internal partitioning, and computer cabling underneath raised floors. There are many examples of break options being defeated by such matters. To take just one, in *Riverside Park Limited v NHS Property Services Limited [2016] EWHC 1313 (Ch)* it was held that a tenant had failed to comply with a vacant possession condition in a break option by leaving demountable partitioning installed within the premises.

An unusual instance of problems arising from a 'vacant possession' condition was provided by *Capitol Park Leeds v Global Radio Services [2021] EWCA Civ 995*. The case concerned a three-storey commercial office property in Leeds, let for a term of 24 years with a tenant's option to break at year 16.

25

The break was conditional, among other things, on the tenant giving vacant possession of 'the Premises', defined so as to include all fixtures and fittings other than tenant's fixtures, and all additions and improvements.

The tenant gave notice to exercise the break, and subsequently carried out a programme of stripping-out works. The parties failed to agree on what elements of the building had formed part of the base build, and what had been installed later, and when it became apparent that a settlement would not be reached, the tenant removed from the building elements including ceiling grids and tiles, fire barriers, floor finishes, window-sills, fan coil units and ductwork, lighting, radiators and pipework.

The Court of Appeal held that the vacant possession condition was not concerned with the physical state of the unit but with whether the landlord was recovering it free of the conventional trilogy of *"people, chattels and interests"*. The condition was not one which required the tenant to have observed and performed their covenants. Moreover, since the yield-up covenant *did* require the premises to be yielded up *"in a state of repair condition and decoration which is consistent with the proper performance of the Tenant's covenants"*, the absence of any such reference in the break clause supported the tenant's interpretation of the break clause.

The condition therefore required the tenant to return 'the Premises' as they were on the break date, free of people, chattels and interests. Whilst the building had been left in a dire state, that did not invalidate the exercise of the break clause, and the landlord's remedy was to seek compensation for whatever loss it may have suffered.

It is precisely in order to avoid this sort of dispute that the *Lease Code* recommends, not a condition for vacant possession, but what might be called a 'vacant possession lite' condition: that the tenant gives up occupation, and leaves no sub-tenants or other occupiers.

Where there is a simple requirement for vacant possession, the tenant should assume that all chattels must be removed. As regards tenant's fixtures, by their nature they *may* be removed by the tenant, but need not be. The tenant should try to agree with the landlord what is to be taken out, but if no agreement can be reached, then a good general rule is for the tenant to remove everything that it is entitled to.

Of course, the tenant must also be sure that any sub-tenants or other occupiers will have left the premises by the break date. The landlord should also be asked where they would like the keys returned.

Condition for payment of premium

A break option is a valuable property right, and this may be reflected in a higher rent being agreed than if there were no break clause, or an agreement that the tenant must pay the landlord a premium, as a condition of exercise of the break.

The mechanics of payment may require attention. There is often an express requirement in the lease for there to be cleared funds in the landlord's account by the break date – even if there is not, it is best to proceed on the basis that that is what should be achieved. The landlord may be content for funds to be paid into a managing agents' account, but any such agreement should be clearly documented.

If the payment method is not specified, the landlord should be asked for written confirmation of what they require. Telegraphic transfers can be subject to delays, and a prudent option is to pay by cheque or banker's draft, sent two weeks early, to give plenty of time to deal with any problems.

Condition for compliance with repair covenants

Disrepair has historically been the most common area of contention; generally the relevant condition will require compliance with all covenants, but disputes tend to centre on the physical condition of the property.

In *Finch v Underwood (1876) 2 Ch D 310*, Mellish LJ observed:

"In a case like this, if a tenant wishes to claim the benefit of such a covenant he should send in his surveyor to see what repairs are needed and should effect the repairs which the surveyor certifies to be requisite. The court would be inclined to give credit to a survey thus honestly made, and would lean towards holding the condition precedent to have been complied with".

Despite that apparently accommodating approach, the disrepair in that case, which would only have cost between £13 and £45 to put right (admittedly in Victorian money), was sufficient to defeat the option.

That passage from *Finch v Underwood* has been quoted with approval in many cases since, right up to the present day, and yet despite tenants following the advice contained in it, break options are regularly defeated by what appear to be minor matters. In *Sirhowy Investments v Henderson [2014] EWHC 3562 (Ch)*, the exercise of the tenants' break option was defeated because they had mended a wooden fence in some places with sheeting panels, instead of restoring it in the original form.

Conditionality on repair has been less of a feature of the caselaw over recent years, perhaps because tenants are getting better at negotiating break clauses. Where a break option is conditional upon repair, it is now common to see the condition qualified to require only 'reasonable', 'substantial' or 'material' compliance.

A condition requiring 'reasonable' compliance was considered in *Gardner v Blaxill [1960] 2 All ER 457*, and the court held that the word *"meant that the tenant could exercise his option provided that he behaved during the tenancy in a way which a reasonably minded tenant might well behave"*. But performance over the whole term is relevant to that assessment, so a breach might defeat the break even though it had been remedied (*Bassett v Whiteley (1982) 45 P&CR 87*). In *Commercial Union v Label Ink [2001] L&TR 380*, it was held that the effect of the word 'reasonably' was that while the tenant did not have to comply fully with the covenants, it did need to show that it had made reasonable efforts to perform them, and it had not.

Other common qualifiers are 'material' or 'substantial' compliance. In *Fitzroy House Epworth Street v Financial Times [2006] 2 All ER 776* the two words were considered to be interchangeable. It was held that the standard of compliance required by such a qualification must be assessed by reference to the landlord's ability to re-let or sell the premises without delay or additional expense.

Tenants should expect to carry out any required repairs even though the landlord may not serve a schedule of dilapidations. The tenant's obligation is to keep the property in repair throughout the term, not to react to a schedule. Equally, if a schedule has been served, the tenant should not assume that compliance is defined by reference to the scheduled items. Some disrepair may have been overlooked, or even deliberately omitted. The tenant should do an independent survey as well, as stated in *Finch v Underwood*.

Anecdotally, landlords may find items of disrepair, enabling them to challenge the exercise of break options, by measures such as CCTV drainage surveys. In a whole building lease, the drains will typically be included within the demise, there is often some defect in them, and the tenant is likely to have overlooked them in addressing issues of repair. Tenants should (as always when dealing with disrepair) consider carefully the extent of the demise.

Turning to decorating obligations, they will often require work in the last year of the term, whether or not it is determined early. If so, service by the tenant of a break notice itself creates an obligation to decorate, prior to the break date. *Osborne Assets v Britannia Life (1997) (Liverpool County Court, unreported)* is a well-known example of the court holding that the break option had been defeated because the decorating condition had not been complied with. This was a case where the tenant complied to the letter with the *Finch v Underwood* advice, and indeed left the property in a state of repair such that the landlord could not find any fault, upon a visual inspection. However, documentation of the tenant's programme of repairs included a decorator's invoice recording that the interior of the property had been decorated with two coats of paint, instead of the three required by the lease. Courts regard decorating covenants seriously, and non-compliance with them has defeated breaks on several occasions.

Some matters may require landlord's approval, for example paint colours. The tenant should of course seek approval early. If the landlord does not respond (landlords are not obliged to assist tenants to exercise their break options), then the tenant must do the best it can.

Obligations to reinstate alterations may be dependent on the landlord notifying a requirement to reinstate. Many leases do not specify a deadline for the landlord to raise such a requirement, and the current caselaw suggests that in the absence of a time limit, the landlord can raise a valid reinstatement requirement right up to expiry of the term, even where it is clearly far too late for the tenant to be able to comply (e.g. *Scottish Mutual Assurance Society v British Telecommunications Plc (1994) (High Court, unreported)* No reported case on validity of a break option has ever turned on a last-minute reinstatement requirement, but the tenant should ask the landlord's intentions in plenty of time, and stand ready to deal with any late reinstatement requirements as far as possible.

Purchasing the risk

It is of course possible to agree terms of settlement with the landlord, so as to avoid the risk of non-compliance. However, tenants should beware distraction and delay; the best approach is to set a timetable for settlement, and stick to it.

In *Legal & General Assurance Society v Expeditors International [2006] 18 EG 151 (CS)*, the parties had settled the dilapidations liability, but the tenant then failed to satisfy the condition for vacant possession. However, the effect of the settlement was held to be that the landlord had waived compliance with the remaining conditions of the break clause. That was a matter of construction of the particular agreement, and will not always apply.

Summary

- Periodic business tenancies must always fall within the 1954 Act. A tenant's notice to quit will terminate a periodic tenancy without the need for any further action under the Act.

  Commonly, commercial periodic tenancies are yearly, and this will mean that, under the common law rule, from six to twelve months' notice to terminate is required, depending on the date from which the tenancy year runs, and when the notice is given. However, an express contractual provision for length of notice will take precedence over the common law rule.

  In the case of an implied periodic tenancy, it can be difficult to be certain of the date from which the tenancy year runs, and what is the appropriate address for service of the notice to quit. Service of multiple notices by multiple methods is sometime necessary.

- Service of a tenant's break notice, like a notice to quit under a periodic tenancy, terminates the tenancy with no need for anything else to be done under the 1954 Act.

  Difficulties in exercising break options frequently arise because of conditions which the tenant is required to satisfy.

  o A condition that rent must be paid up to date at the break date will often mean, in the absence of appropriate provision for apportionment in the lease, that on the final rent day the tenant must pay a full quarter's rent, even though it will not be entitled to a full quarter's possession.

  o A condition that all payments must be paid up to date presents considerable practical difficulties, and tenants may need to be prepared to over-pay, and reclaim the excess later.

o   Conditions that vacant possession must be given raise issues about the tenant removing chattels and tenant's fixtures from the premises, and tenants must be prepared to remove everything, unless the landlord agrees otherwise.

o   If there is a condition for payment of a premium by the tenant, attention must be paid to the timing and method of payment.

o   Unqualified conditions that the tenant must have complied with its covenants can raise difficult issues about the state of repair of the property, particularly in relation to reinstatement and decorating obligations.

CHAPTER THREE

OTHER MODES OF TERMINATION OUTSIDE THE 1954 ACT

This chapter considers termination of a licence to occupy, a tenancy at will, a six-month tenancy, and a contracted-out tenancy. In each case, termination is effected without employing any procedure under the 1954 Act. Termination of tenancies by surrender is also covered.

There is a range of methods by which tenants can terminate tenancies which are protected by the Landlord and Tenant Act 1954. The applicable methods vary as between different types of tenancy, and vary also on a chronological basis, depending on the point in the lease term at which termination is to be effected, and the progress which has been made in the procedure under the Act. Further, although a tenancy may be within the 1954 Act, it must be validly terminated by the appropriate contractual method as well as the appropriate statutory one. It is because this presents rather a complex picture that the main focus of this book is on termination under the 1954 Act.

However, many tenants will occupy pursuant to tenancies or other occupational arrangements which fall outside the Act, and in this chapter we consider termination of those arrangements.

Termination of licence to occupy

A licence to occupy is a contractual permission to occupy property. So is a tenancy; either type of arrangement results in one party in occupation of another party's land, and (usually) paying for the privilege. The difference is that grant of a tenancy creates a legal interest in land, while a licence to occupy does not. The key to the licence/tenancy distinction is whether, as a matter of fact, the occupier has been granted exclusive possession of the premises. If there is exclusive possession, it is a tenancy, if not, it is some other sort of occupational arrangement, typically a licence to occupy.

Following the House of Lords decision in *Street v Mountford [1985] UKHL 4*, in any dispute the courts will examine the transaction to determine whether or not the parties have actually created a tenancy, despite using a form of document which states that it is a licence to occupy. If the occupier has in fact been granted exclusive possession, then the document will be considered to have created a tenancy. A genuine licence to occupy, exactly because it is not a tenancy, will fall outside the scope of the 1954 Act.

Landlords therefore sometimes try to avoid conferring security of tenure by granting a licence to occupy in preference to a tenancy. Many landlords and their agents have standard form so-called 'letter licences': one- or two-page agreements in letter form, which they use to document short periods of occupation. In sectors such as serviced offices and co-working, occupational documents may be called 'property supply agreements', or 'serviced office agreements', or some such, but on analysis they are commonly licences to occupy. Agreements for lease may often specify that where the tenant is permitted access to the premises ahead of completion of the lease, in order to fit out, their occupation will be in the capacity of licensee.

Licences may also arise by implication, in circumstances where occupation is not the subject of any express agreement between the property-owner and the occupier (for example, *Vaughan v Vaughan [1953] 1 QB 762*).

Whether a licence is express or implied, identifying the means of termination does not involve any consideration of the Landlord and Tenant Act 1954, since it does not apply. Where the document arguably gives rise to a tenancy, however, the various means of termination of tenancies will be relevant, and may obviously include termination under the 1954 Act.

As regards express licences to occupy, there will generally be provision governing means of termination, involving a short notice period, and usually without any significant formality attached to the giving of notice. Of course, if there is any formality required by the agreement it must be observed.

In the case of an implied licence, or an express one which does not specify a notice period, caselaw governing the required length of notice has been concerned with notices given by the property-owner, not by the occupier. It has been held that the licensee must be given a reasonable time to vacate (*Minister of Health v Bellotti [1944] KB 298*; *Vaughan v Vaughan [1953] 1 QB 762*). In the case of notice given by the licensee, while there seems to be no authority on the point, there is a case for requiring a short reasonable period of notice likewise, so that the owner can make arrangements for insurance cover, security, utilities and so forth.

A fixed-period licence will of course come to an end on the date stated. Since there can be no security of tenure, no action to terminate will be required on the part of either owner or occupier.

Termination of tenancy at will

A tenancy at will is a hybrid creature, whose legal origins lie in the concept of the licence to occupy. However, it is now a distinct form of occupation, a type of tenancy, under which the occupier has exclusive possession. Its essential characteristic is that it lasts 'at the will' of both parties; that is, it will come to an end immediately upon one party notifying the other to that effect.

Tenancies at will most often arise by implication, however they can be and are created expressly, and usually the reason is to avoid security of tenure under the 1954 Act. In the same way that landlords and their agents have standard form 'letter licences', they may also have standard form tenancy at will agreements.

It is established by caselaw that the 1954 Act does not apply to tenancies at will, whether arising by implication of law (*Wheeler v Mercer [1957] AC 416*), or expressly (*Hagee (London) Ltd v AB Erikson and Larson [1976] QB 209*). As with a licence to occupy, the courts will examine the reality of the transaction to identify whether a tenancy at will has genuinely been granted. It is easier to ensure a genuine tenancy at will than a genuine licence to occupy, though, since there is no need to establish that exclusive possession has not been granted. Instead, the issue is whether the agreement includes any terms inconsistent with the notion of a tenancy which is terminable at any time without notice (*Binion v Evans [1972] 2 All ER 70*).

A tenancy at will must be determinable at the will of either party, and because the precarious nature of that arrangement is inconvenient and risky, the parties are often tempted to 'improve' upon it by agreeing terms which modify the position. The kind of terms to avoid, because they would be inconsistent with a tenancy at will, would include:

- a fixed term or specified minimum period

- a period of notice for termination

- a clause prohibiting or restricting assignment or sub-letting. This would conflict with the nature of a tenancy at will as a personal arrangement between landlord and tenant, which cannot be assigned or sub-let

- a forfeiture clause. A tenancy at will can be terminated forthwith, with no security of tenure, and so there is no need for a forfeiture provision

Payment of rent in advance *may* indicate that the tenancy is intended to be for a minimum term, or is to be periodic, and so *may* indicate that the agreement is not a tenancy at will. However, that is only one indicator, and so long as the document is otherwise unproblematic, a tenancy at will agreement can certainly provide for rent payable in advance. Where it does so, though, the terms of the agreement should provide for repayment of any sum that is attributable to a period after the tenancy is brought to an end.

Assuming that the arrangement is genuinely a tenancy at will, whether express or implied the means of termination is identical, and very straightforward. The tenant need only notify the landlord that the tenancy is at an end with immediate effect. As with a licence to occupy, should there be any prescribed formality then it must be observed, but there rarely is.

Termination of six-month tenancy

The operation of *s.43(3)* of the 1954 Act was outlined in the previous chapter: tenancies for six months or less fall outside the Act, although there is an exception to this rule in favour of tenants who have accrued twelve months' continuous business occupation, who therefore have security of tenure even if occupying under a tenancy for six months or less.

It is for this reason that it is common to find licences to occupy granted for six months. In such a case, even if the occupier actually enjoys exclusive possession, so that a court would find the agreement to be a tenancy, there would be no security of tenure. One may ask why not give the arrangement its correct description as a tenancy, if that is what it is in reality, and indeed some landlords whose aim is to avoid conferring security of tenure will let on successive six-month leases, in reliance on *s.43(3)*.

The difficulty is that the effectiveness of this strategy for avoiding security is time-limited because of the 'twelve months' occupation' exception. An additional complication is that the Act does not specify whether the length of occupation is assessed for this purpose at the beginning or end of the tenancy. Take the example of a landlord who grants three successive tenancies of five months to the same tenant. The first two tenancies are unproblematic: they are granted for less than six months, and the tenant at no time has more than twelve months' occupation. As regards the third tenancy, though, there are three possibilities:

- The tenancy is within the Act, because when it terminates the tenant will have been in occupation for fifteen months

- The tenancy falls outside the Act, because when it is granted the tenant has been in occupation for only ten months

- The tenancy is outside the Act when granted, but comes within the Act as soon as the tenant has had a total of twelve months' occupation

There is no authority to indicate which of these is correct, though some respected commentators have given it as their view that the third tenancy would be outside the Act. However, the only safe policy for a landlord who wishes to grant leases outside the 1954 Act is to grant successive tenancies of no more than six months, totalling no more than twelve months..

Assuming a tenancy of six months or less, falling outside the Act by virtue of *s.43(3)*, it will of course come to an end on its expiry date in the same way as a fixed-period licence. Since there is no security of tenure, no action to terminate will be required on the part of either landlord or tenant.

Termination of contracted-out tenancies

A contracted-out tenancy is another type of arrangement which simply comes to an end at the stated expiry date, with no action required on either side. It may of course contain a break option, in which case notice must be served if it is to be terminated on the break date.

Consideration may have to be given as to whether the contracting-out procedure has been correctly followed, since an invalid contracting-out would result in a tenancy with security of tenure.

Summary of the contracting-out procedure

The present contracting-out procedure was introduced by the *Regulatory Reform (Business Tenancies) (England and Wales) Order 2003 (SI 2003/3096)* ("the 2003 Order"), in substitution for the previous court-based process, and it came into effect in 2004. In essence, it is very simple. It has three stages, which must be done in the following order:

- The landlord sends the tenant a warning notice drawing the tenant's attention to the protection which it will be signing away;

- The tenant makes a formal declaration to the effect that it has read and understood the notice;

- The parties sign a lease containing the contracting-out agreement.

The correct prescribed forms of notice and declaration must be used.

The notice and declaration must be exchanged before the tenant has become contractually bound – so for example, if there is a prior agreement for lease, they must have been exchanged before the tenant enters into the agreement for lease.

Tenancy for a term of years certain

As noted in the previous chapter, under *s.38A* it is only tenancies "for a term of years certain" which can be contracted-out.

- An obvious consequence is that a periodic tenancy cannot be contracted-out.

- Another aspect of the restriction was explored in *Receiver for the Metropolitan Police District v Palacegate Properties Ltd [2000] EWCA Civ 33*, where it was argued that a fixed-term lease which incorporated a break clause was not a tenancy for a term of years certain, and therefore could not validly be contracted-out. That argument was rejected by the Court of Appeal, and it is clear that the inclusion of a break clause does not prevent contracting-out.

- The case on this point which took most practitioners by surprise was that of *London Borough of Newham v Thomas-Van Staden [2008] EWCA Civ 1414*. For reasons relating to the old rule of privity of contract, leases often define "the Term" to include not only the fixed period, but also "*any continuation, extension or holding over*". Of course, a contracted-out lease would have no such period of continuation, so that wording would be inappropriate and unnecessary in such a lease. In the *Thomas-Van Staden* case, that wording had been included in a contracted-out lease, obviously by oversight. The Court of Appeal took the view that as a consequence the term was not a "term of years certain", and accordingly the lease was not validly contracted-out.

There is much to criticise in the decision; nevertheless, for the present at least it remains the law. The upshot is that the definition of the term in a contracted-out lease should not include any extension, continuation or holding-over period, and if it does then the lease is not validly contracted-out.

When should the notice be served?

Under the old court-based procedure, it was a requirement of the court rules that the agreed form of lease should be attached to the documents submitted to court. Under the present procedure, some practitioners consider it is still best practice to attach the agreed form of lease to the notice, to help in putting together the paper trail demonstrating that there has been an effective contracting-out.

Those who take this cautious approach cannot, it follows, serve the notice until the form of lease is finalised, or almost finalised. Taking the more robust view, the notice may be served earlier than that, even right at the outset, as soon as heads of terms have been agreed, and many practitioners are comfortable with that practice. Serving earlier has at least the advantage of giving more time to deal with any problems in obtaining the appropriate declaration from the tenant.

There has not as yet been any challenge to the validity of a contracting-out process based on a failure to attach the agreed form of lease to a notice, or on the timing of service. It is suggested that any such challenge would be unlikely to succeed.

Simple declaration or statutory declaration?

Under *Schedule 2* to the 2003 Order, the tenant's declaration made in response to the warning notice may be either a statutory declaration made under the *Statutory Declarations Act 1835*, or a 'simple' declaration, made without that degree of formality. The two prescribed forms of declaration are identical in substance, the only difference being that the form of statutory declaration has the required statutory formalities at the end of the document, and is witnessed by a solicitor for a £5 fee.

If the tenant makes a statutory declaration, the lease can be executed without delay; if the tenant makes a simple declaration, the lease must be executed not less than 14 days after service of the notice, and if it is executed earlier than that, then the lease will not be validly contracted-out. The statutory declaration procedure is invariably adopted in practice. Practitioners usually see no benefit in using the simple declaration when that might delay completion of the transaction.

One issue which had not been anticipated came before the courts in the case of *Chiltern Railway Company Ltd v Patel [2008] EWCA Civ 178*: if a statutory declaration has been used, but in the event the tenant executes the lease more than 14 days after the notice, so that a simple declaration would have sufficed, is the contracting-out valid? The Court of Appeal had no difficulty in deciding that it was.

Unrepresented tenants

Very many small businesses, on taking a lease of business premises, manage without professional advice, to save on fees. This can give rise to a practical problem for landlords: even though it has been provided with the correct form, the tenant may not complete the declaration correctly (sometimes a problem even where the tenant does have legal representation). A common issue is the tenant just signing the declaration, rather than taking it to a solicitor to have it administered as a statutory declaration. If the tenant cannot be persuaded to complete this formality properly, then there is at least the option of accepting it as a simple declaration, waiting 14 days, and then completing the lease.

As regards any other errors, the landlord must insist that the declaration is completed to its satisfaction before the lease can be completed, and the tenant given access to the premises.

Stating the term commencement date in the declaration

Both forms of declaration require that some details as to the intended tenancy be set out. The only aspect of that requirement which potentially causes difficulties is that the term commencement date must be specified. This is not always possible; it may be the date of execution of the lease, or it may depend on fulfilment of some condition, such as obtaining superior landlord's consent. All that can be done in those circumstances is to describe how the term commencement date is to be arrived at, for example:

- *"a term commencing on the execution of the lease"*; or

- *"a term commencing on the date to be inserted at clause [ ] of the lease"*; or

- *"a term commencing on a date to be agreed"*

Some have doubted whether that complies with the requirements of *Schedule 2* to the 2003 Order, but the purpose of giving the required information in the declaration is to identify the transaction to which the notice and declaration relate, and so long as the description used fulfils that purpose as best it can, then the contracting-out should be valid: *TFS Stores Ltd v BMG (Ashford) Ltd [2021] EWCA Civ 688.*

Steps taken by solicitors or agents

If a letting agent, or a solicitor, serves the warning notice on behalf of the landlord, that would generally be considered to be within the scope of their usual role, and so they should not need to verify that they have the landlord's express authority to do so.

The position is different if the notice is to be served upon anyone other than the tenant itself: receiving notices is not considered to fall with the scope of the authority usually enjoyed by a solicitor or letting agent (*Re Munro [1981] 3 All ER 215*). Some verification of authority should therefore be sought, before serving the warning notice on them. Some practitioners will always serve notice on the tenant itself, even if assured that the tenant's solicitor has express actual authority to receive the notice. Most, though, will serve on the tenant's solicitor if assured that express actual authority has been given.

Equally, the declaration may be made by someone on the tenant's behalf, and if so then their actual express authority to do so should be verified.

Such doubts as there may have been on these points have largely been allayed by the first-instance decision in *TFS Stores Ltd v BMG (Ashford) Ltd [2019] EWHC 1363 (Ch)*. In that case, a multiple retailer sought to establish that six of its leases, entered into with the same landlord, were within the 1954 Act, despite having in each case gone through the contracting-out procedure. On the evidence the court had no difficulty in finding that the tenant's solicitors and employees with whom the landlord dealt had the requisite authority to receive notices and make declarations. This conclusion must depend on the specific factual background, but it is likely to be very difficult for a tenant to succeed in establishing an absence of authority in a situation where the landlord has dealt in good faith with the tenant's representatives who have been given conduct of lease negotiations and implementation.

If the contracting-out is invalid

To summarise this brief discussion of the contracting-out process, the most dependable reasons for a lease not being validly contracted-out (some of which are quite unlikely to occur in practice) are:

a) Notice and declaration having been made after execution of the lease (or agreement for lease)

b) Declaration having been made before service of the notice

c) Notice or declaration not having been made in the prescribed form

d) The definition of "the Term" in the lease having been drafted so as to include any extension, continuation or holding-over period

e) The Lease failing to contain the required recital of the exchange of notice and declaration, and/or the agreement to contract the lease out of the Act.

If the applicable reason in any particular case is (a), (b), (c) or (e), the tenant will need to operate the termination procedures under the 1954 Act, as discussed in Chapters 5 to 9.

If (d) applies, the tenant is presented with something of a puzzle.

- To terminate the tenancy under the Act it would be necessary to serve on the landlord a request for a new tenancy under *s.26* (discussed in Chapter 7), or a notice to terminate under *s.27(1)* or *s.27(2)* (see Chapters 5 and 6), or to go out of occupation before the contractual expiry date pursuant to *s.27(1A)* (Chapter 8).

- None of those procedures is possible unless the contractual expiry date can be identified, but because the impact of *London Borough of Newham v Thomas-Van Staden [2008] EWCA Civ 1414* is that a lease so drafted is not a tenancy for a term of years certain, it is difficult to see how it can be identified.

The implication is that the tenancy cannot be terminated, and will continue indefinitely. This analysis conflicts with the rule that there can be no tenancy unless the term is certain or can be rendered certain (*Prudential Assurance Co Ltd v London Residuary Body [1992] 3 All ER 504 (HL)*).

The answer may be that, as in the *Prudential* case, occupation and payment of rent give rise to an implied periodic tenancy, in which case termination would be effected as discussed in the previous chapter.

Lease surrender

Under *s.24(2)* of the 1954 Act, surrender is one of the common law methods of lease termination which remains effective. It follows that if a lease is terminated by being surrendered, no continuation tenancy under *s.24(1)* will arise, and neither party is entitled to invoke the renewal process under the Act by service of a *s.25* notice or *s.26* request.

Unlike the other methods of lease termination discussed in this book, surrender cannot be effected unilaterally by the tenant (or landlord, for that matter). The essence of surrender is agreement: the parties have agreed that the lease should come to an end. This does not necessarily mean that the landlord will recover vacant possession, since any sub-leases will remain extant and in full effect after surrender of a headlease.

Surrender by deed

A surrender may of course be documented in a surrender deed. Indeed, in any but the most straightforward circumstances, there will usually be a need to document the terms which the parties have negotiated. This is particularly the case where multiple parties need to be involved: for example there are joint tenants (or landlords), or there are guarantors to be released from their liabilities.

A deed, rather than a simple contract, is required because the tenant is conveying the lease term to the landlord (*s.52(1)*, *Law of Property Act 1925*, *Crago v Julian [1992] 1 All ER 744*). However, if a document other than a deed is used, it may still take effect as a surrender 'by operation of law'.

Surrender by operation of law

There is potential uncertainty in going down the route of surrender by operation of law, at least by comparison with the certainty offered by an express surrender deed.

A surrender of a lease by operation of law occurs where the actions of the parties demonstrate that they intend to bring a lease to an end. As with all matters of contract, it is of course the 'objective intention' which is relevant, rather than the 'subjective intention'; in other words, intention as observed from the actions and statements of the parties, and not from their testimony as to what was in their mind at the time.

A straightforward and traditional way of effecting surrender by operation of law is for the tenant to hand back to the landlord the keys to the premises, together with the original lease. When the landlord accepts them, both parties have demonstrated an unequivocal intention to treat the lease as terminated. This was a popular method of effecting surrenders before Stamp Duty was replaced by Stamp Duty Land Tax in 2003. There is often a premium payable on a surrender, and Stamp Duty might well be payable on the transaction when the document was produced for stamping. Stamp Duty, however, was a tax on documents: no document, no tax. So, prior to 2003, many surrenders were effected informally, by operation of law, so as to avoid paying Stamp Duty. Stamp Duty Land Tax, by contrast, is a tax on transactions, whether or not documented in a written agreement, so that it is payable regardless of how the surrender is effected.

Up to 2003, before the reform of land registration law and practice in the *Land Registration Act 2002*, it was generally only necessary to register a lease if it was for a term of 21 years or more. That meant that there were no Land Registry complications to arise as a result of accepting informal surrenders of leases in this way. The introduction of Stamp Duty Land Tax roughly coincided with the coming into force of the *Land Registration Act 2002*, upon which leases of seven years or more became registrable, and the two developments together made surrender by operation of law much less attractive.

Consent of chargee

If a lease is charged, termination of the lease by surrender will destroy the chargee's security. It follows that the surrender cannot take effect unless the chargee has consented to it.

Surrender where tenant is insolvent

It is not infrequently the case that the reason for a landlord accepting a surrender is that the tenant is insolvent, and where the insolvency takes the form of a winding-up, the liquidator must obtain a court order authorising the surrender. Under *s.127, Insolvency Act 1986*, any disposition of a company's property made after the presentation of a winding-up petition is void unless done with the court's authority.

In *OfficeServe Technologies Ltd v Anthony-Mike [2017] EWHC 1920 (Ch)* the court endorsed the conventional view, as expressed by Lord Neuberger in *Akers v Samba Financial Group [2017] UKSC 6*, that a lease surrender falls within *s.127*.

The equivalent provision as regards bankruptcy of individual tenants is *s.248(1)* of the *Insolvency Act 1986*.

As regards companies in administration, the administrator's consent to a lease surrender is required under *Schedule B1, para.64(1)*, while the administrator himself has power to surrender a lease under *Schedule 1, para.17*.

Matters for negotiation

Because a surrender is a consensual process, the range of matters which fall for consideration on lease expiry, such as dilapidations, reinstatement of alterations, etc., are all open for negotiation. The usual common law consequences need not follow, therefore, but can be modified by the parties' agreement.

The outcome of the negotiation will depend, as ever, upon the bargaining position of the parties. A tenant with a strong incentive to terminate its rental commitment in relation to the premises is likely to be prepared to make concessions; the same applies to a landlord with a priority need to obtain vacant possession.

If there are not too many matters to be agreed, it may be possible to document them in a simple agreement, or exchange of letters, and proceed to a surrender by operation of law. The lengthier and more detailed the terms, of course, the more an express surrender deed is indicated.

Summary

Other than termination by contractual notice (covered in Chapter 2), there are a number of ways in which a tenant may terminate a business tenancy outside the Landlord and Tenant Act 1954.

If occupation is documented by means of a licence to occupy, the 1954 Act does not apply. A fixed-period licence will come to an end on the date stated. In the case of an express licence to occupy, there may be provision for termination by notice, and this will be effective so long as the contractual terms are observed. In the case of an implied licence, or an express one which does not specify a notice period, a court is likely to consider that a short reasonable period of notice is required to terminate.

If the tenant holds under a tenancy at will, the 1954 Act does not apply. To terminate, the tenant need only notify the landlord that the tenancy is at an end with immediate effect.

If the tenant has a contracted-out tenancy, it will simply come to an end at the expiry date, and no action is required by either party. It may contain a break option, in which case notice must be served if it is to be terminated on the break date. Consideration may have to be given as to whether the contracting-out procedure has been correctly followed, since the tenancy will not be contracted-out if it has not.

With the landlord's agreement, tenancies may also be terminated by surrender. This is conventionally done by way of a surrender deed, though it may alternatively be done informally by delivery of the lease and the keys. Consent of any holder of a charge over the lease is required, and if the tenant is in an insolvency procedure, consent of the office-holder may be needed.

CHAPTER FOUR

GENERAL GUIDANCE ON DRAFTING AND SERVICE OF NOTICES

This chapter considers the practicalities involved in drafting and serving a valid notice.

Many of the termination procedures covered in this book involve service of a notice. While notices are intended to bring certainty into legal relations, drafting and serving one is a formal, technical action, and it is striking how many disputes come before the courts which concern the validity of notices.

A valid notice must:

- Convey the appropriate meaning to implement the contractual or statutory provision under which it is served

- Comply with any prescribed formalities

- Contain any information which it is required to contain

- Be served in the prescribed manner

- Be served in accordance with any applicable time limits

- Be served at the correct place

- Be served on the correct recipient

- Be served by the correct sender

As regards most items on that list, there is no flexibility: if the notice is defective in respect of any such item, then it is not a valid notice. It is only as regards the first, and the last two, items that the courts have been prepared to take a more flexible approach. That flexibility derives from the leading case of *Mannai Investment Co Ltd v Eagle Star Life Assurance Co Ltd [1997] AC 749*.

The *Mannai* approach

In that case, two leases each contained a break clause enabling the tenant to determine the lease "*by serving not less than six months' notice in writing ... such notice to expire on the third anniversary of the term commencement date*'. The tenant purported to give notice to determine the leases on 12 January 1995, although the third anniversary of the commencement date was in fact 13 January 1995. The House of Lords held (by a majority) that the notices were valid.

The majority considered that where a tenant served a notice purporting to exercise its contractual right to determine a lease, that notice would be effective to do so notwithstanding the fact that it contained a minor misdescription, provided that, construed against its contextual setting, it would unambiguously inform a reasonable recipient how and when it was to operate. Having regard to the fact that the leases commenced on 13 January and were determinable on the third anniversary of the term commencement, it would have been obvious to a reasonable recipient that the notices contained a minor misdescription, and that the tenant sought to determine the leases on "*the third anniversary of the term commencement*", i.e. 13 January.

Lord Steyn explained:

> "*The question is not whether 12 January can mean 13 January: it self-evidently cannot. The real question is a different one: does the notice construed against its contextual setting unambiguously inform a reasonable recipient how and when the notice is to operate under the right reserved?*"

The approach applies not only to contractual notices, but also to statutory ones: *York v Casey [1998] 2 EGLR 25* and *Speedwell Estates Ltd v Dalziel [2001] EWCA Civ 1277*. In the case of a statutory notice, it is also necessary to consider whether the notice complies with the relevant statutory requirements, bearing in mind their purpose. Even if a notice does not precisely comply with the statutory requirements, it may be possible to conclude that it is *"substantially to the same effect"* as a prescribed form, if it nevertheless fulfils the statutory purpose (*Pease v Carter [2020] EWCA Civ 175*).

Mannai has rescued many defective notices in reported cases. For example, in *Tyco Fire & Integrated Solutions (UK) Ltd v Regent Quay Development Company Ltd [2016] CSOH 97*, a break notice should have referred to three units within a commercial property, which were all held on the same lease; by mistake it referred only to two of them. The court considered, applying *Mannai*, that the reasonable recipient would not have been misled and that the notice was valid.

However, the approach is not applicable to pure questions of the required form of the document. In Lord Hoffmann's well-known words:

> *"If the clause had said that the notice had to be on blue paper, it would have been no good serving a notice on pink paper, however clear it might have been that the tenant wanted to terminate the lease."*

In *Friends Life Ltd v Siemens Hearing Instruments Ltd [2014] EWCA Civ 382*, the break clause stated that any break notice *"must be expressed to be given under the Landlord and Tenant Act 1954, s.24(2)"*. That requirement made some sense when the lease was drafted, but the High Court decision in *Garston v Scottish Widows Fund and Life Assurance Society [1998] 1 WLR 1583* rendered it effectively pointless. So when it came to preparing and serving the break notice, the tenant omitted any reference to *s.24(2)* of the Act. In all other respects the notice complied perfectly with the requirements of the lease. It was held to be an invalid notice, as this was not a question of whether the meaning of the notice was unclear or misleading, but whether it complied with the required formalities. Matters of form must be strictly complied with.

Lord Steyn, in his judgment in *Mannai*, addressed the question of whether the new flexibility would 'open the floodgates' to a rush of cases on the validity of notices. He said:

> "*That brings me to counsel's argument that, if the notices are treated as valid, there will be a great deal of confusion and unnecessary litigation. Experience teaches that 'floodgates' arguments need to be examined with an initial scepticism. In this case the predictions of counsel are unrealistic.*"

He may have been unduly sanguine: a search on a well-known legal database using the search term 'Mannai' produces hundreds of results.

One of the problems is that it is not always obvious whether the question is to do with the meaning conveyed by the notice (in which case *Mannai* applies), or the required formalities or content (in which case *Mannai* does not apply).

Leases are sometimes encountered in which the form of break notice is set out in a schedule, and in that instance, at least, the position is clear: following the prescribed form is a matter of formality, not content, and any departure from it will invalidate the notice.

Drafting for *Mannai*

In drafting a notice, although human errors such as mis-identifying the property will always occur, the risk of invalidity can be much reduced by bearing in mind the *Mannai* approach. The objective is to produce a document that cannot leave a reasonable recipient in any doubt as to what it is trying to do. Good general rules are:

- A notice is something which notifies. Use an expression such as "*Take notice that …*", "*You are hereby notified that …*", or "*We hereby give you notice that …*".

- Identify the lease and the clause number. A document which says "*Pursuant to clause 4(3) of a lease dated 25 March 2012 and made between (1) A Limited (2) B Limited and (3) B Parent Plc you are hereby notified that...*" cannot easily give rise to any confusion as to what the sender is trying to do.

- Track the clause wording as necessary. If the clause says that "*the Tenant may terminate the lease by not less than six months' notice expiring on 25 March 2017*", then the notice should be along the lines of "*...we hereby give you notice, being not less than six months' notice, to terminate the lease on 25 March 2017*"

- Include no more information than is required – extraneous information may throw doubt on whether the intention is to give the required notice. If more information has to be given, put it in a covering letter, or even a completely separate letter. Beware contradiction: for example, a notice terminating a lease, accompanied by correspondence purporting to require the recipient to do something which could be regarded as referable to a continuation of the lease.

- Do not use headings such as "*subject to contract*" or "*without prejudice*", which risk a finding that the notice was not intended to have any legal effect – although *Royal Life Insurance v Phillips [1990] 2 EGLR 135* is a rare example of a notice being held valid despite having both those headings.

Required information

Generally, if a contract or statute requires that a notice contain certain information, a notice which does not contain that information will not be valid. *Burman v Mount Cook Land [2001] EWCA Civ 1712* was a case concerning a tenant of a flat under a long lease at a low rent serving notice to acquire a new lease, under the *Leasehold Reform, Housing and Urban Development Act 1993*. The landlord's counter-notice failed to state, as required under *s.45(2)* of that Act, whether the landlord did or did not admit that the tenant had on the relevant date the right to acquire a new lease of the flat, or which (if any) of the proposals contained in the tenant's notice were accepted by the landlord. It was held not to be a valid notice. That is an instance of a failure to comply with a statutory scheme, but the same principle carries over to the contractual context.

The Commercial Court decision in *Ipsos SA v Dentsu Aegis Network Ltd [2015] EWHC 1171 (Comm)* concerned a clause in a share purchase agreement dealing with notification of claims by the buyer against the seller for breach of warranty. In a number of respects the purported claim notice failed to contain the requisite information, and it was therefore held not to be a valid notice. The buyer lost out on several potential claims as a result.

A particular issue in relation to required information arises where the notice must propose a price. *Viscount Chelsea v Morris [1999] 1 EGLR 59* concerned the statutory entitlement of tenants to purchase the freehold of their properties, again under the *Leasehold Reform, Housing and Urban Development Act 1993*. The tenant served a notice to acquire, proposing a nominal price of £100, when the true value would have been much higher. The court held that to be effective a notice must be a genuine notice, and that in order to be genuine it must quote a realistic price. The case did not purport to lay down any general principle, but it is one to be borne in mind when specifying rental figures in rent review or lease renewal notices.

Manner of service

The procedural considerations involved in effecting service correctly are numerous.

Requirement for writing

Some notices may be given orally, but this is unusual. Leases will generally require that notice be given in writing. Under the *Interpretation Act 1978, Sched 1*, writing *"includes typing, printing, lithography, photography and other modes of representing or reproducing words in a visible form"*. This probably includes fax transmission: *PNC Telecom v Geremy Thomas [2003] BCC 202* (the case concerned service of a notice under a company's articles of association). Whether it includes e-mail is debatable. These issues may be addressed in modern leases; for example, some standard boilerplate notice clauses provide options to allow for service by fax and e-mail, with appropriate safeguards to deal with bounce-backs etc..

Signature

As regards signature of the notice, there is usually no problem with the notice having been signed by an agent for the serving party. However, unusually, the court may find that a specific type of notice must be signed by the party in person, as was the case in *Hilmi v 20 Pembridge Villas Freehold Ltd [2010] EWCA Civ 314*. The case concerned the statutory scheme under the *Leasehold Reform, Housing and Urban Development Act 1993*, and turned upon peculiarities of the drafting of that Act.

The court remarked that counsel's researches had turned up only one other, equally obscure, example of a provision requiring signature by a party itself, and not by an agent. Of course, signature by a company cannot be effected personally, so in that rare case where personal signature only will suffice, and where the signing party is a company, it was held in *Hilmi* that the formalities for signature of contracts by companies, contained in *Companies Act 2006, s.44*, apply equally to notices.

Must notice be received?

Generally, for a notice to have been effectively served it must actually have been received by the intended recipient: *Beanby Estates v Egg Stores [2003] 1 WLR 2064*. The case concerned a specific statutory scheme under *s.23, Landlord and Tenant Act 1927*, and decided that under *s.23* a notice could be validly served *without* having actually been received. However, the court reviewed the authorities on service of notices exhaustively, and confirmed the general common law rule that a notice must be received.

Service by or on agent

Service *by* an agent is generally possible: *Galinski v McHugh [1988] 57 P&CR 359*, but before serving *on* an agent it is necessary to check that they do in fact have sufficient authority. The remark made in *Re Munro [1981] 3 All ER 215*, as regards sending notice to a party's solicitor, should be borne in mind:

> "*It is, of course, a common fallacy to think that solicitors have an implied authority on behalf of their clients to receive notices. They may have express authority so to receive them, but in general a solicitor does not have any authority to accept a notice on behalf of his client*"

It follows that it is prudent to obtain confirmation of actual express authority before serving on an agent. *Holwell Securities v Hughes [1974] 1 WLR 155* is an example of lack of authority invalidating service. Notice was received by the defendant's solicitors, who did not in fact have authority to receive the notice, but who told the defendant they had been served with it. The court held that the notice was not validly served. The judge commented:

> "*A person does not give notice in writing to another person by sitting down and writing it out and then telephoning to that other saying 'Listen to what I have just written*".

However, in *TFS Stores Ltd v BMG (Ashford) Ltd [2019] EWHC 1363 (Ch)*, the judge was satisfied that the instruction of solicitors to conduct contracting-out procedures on behalf of the tenant conferred both apparent and express authority to receive service of the warning notices. Moreover, in the same case, it was held that service on solicitors of 'double value' notices under *s.1, Landlord and Tenant Act 1730* was valid without any finding of specific authority to receive service. The general instruction to act for the tenant in relation to the lease expiry was sufficient to constitute them as agents for this purpose.

Context is everything, and in that case the solicitors had express authority to deal with (a) contracting-out, and (b) lease expiry, which in each instance was considered to include the specific matter of receiving notices. Equally, in *Townsends Carriers Ltd v Pfizer Ltd (1977) 33 P&CR 361*, there was a history of apparent authority in relation to dealings with a leased property, so that service of notice by a company which was not the tenant, upon a company which was not the landlord, was held to amount to good service by tenant upon landlord.

Another instance of the importance of context is *UKI (Kingsway) Limited (Respondent) v Westminster City Council (Appellant) [2018] UKSC 67*, the relevant factor in this instance being the particular statutory regime. The case was concerned with service by the rating authority of a notice that a new building had been completed, thus triggering liability for non-domestic rates. The notice was not sent to the company which owned the building, but e-mailed to the building's receptionist, employed by the company managing the building. The receptionist was not authorised by either company to receive service.

Nevertheless, the Supreme Court held that service had been validly effected, since the statutory scheme under the *Local Government Finance Act 1988* did not provide that the prescribed means of service were exclusive. The real issue was whether the rating authority had caused the notice to be received by the building's owner, which did not require any conclusions as to which party controlled the actions of the receptionist. It was unnecessary and unrealistic to introduce concepts of agency or statutory delegation.

In the light of these decisions, it may seem like an excess of caution to insist on confirmation of actual authority, but it will not always be straightforward to identify where circumstances permit a more relaxed approach to issues of agency. It remains best practice, where solicitors and/or managing agents are acting for the intended recipient: (a) to serve the notice on the party itself, but copy in the professional advisers as a courtesy; or (b) to obtain written confirmation of the professional advisers' authority to receive service.

Mandatory/directory service clauses

Contracts will generally stipulate how notices are to be sent. Where that is the case, one of the contractual methods of service should be used where possible, and whether or not any other method of service is also used simultaneously. If the contractual method is followed, there can be no dispute as to validity of service. The same applies where methods of service are laid down by statute, not contract.

Where a non-specified method has been used, the question for the court is whether the contractual or statutory provision for a particular method of service is "mandatory" or "directory" – *Orchard (Developments) v Reuters [2009] 16 EG 140*. If it is mandatory, then no other method of service will suffice; if it is directory, then other methods are possible. A mandatory service provision might typically say that "*notice will be validly served only if...*".

It was held in *Warwick Ltd v GPS (Great Britain) Ltd [2006] PLSCS 210* that clear words are needed to exclude common law methods; in other words, the default position is that notice provisions are not mandatory. This applies also where the contract incorporates one of the statutory service schemes by reference. So it will often be possible to serve by a non-specified method where it is not possible to use a specified one, for example where time pressure does not allow postal service.

Statutory provisions as to service of notices

- Under *s.1139, Companies Act 2006*, notices can be served on a company registered in England and Wales by:

  a) Leaving at the company's registered office

  b) Posting to the company's registered office

  The Act makes equivalent provision for overseas companies whose particulars are registered under *s.1146*.

There are two further statutory provisions which apply in the context of property transactions (though any contract may incorporate them by reference).

- Where *s.196, Law of Property Act 1925* applies, notices may be served by:

a) Leaving at the recipient's last-known place of abode or business

b) Sending by registered or recorded delivery to the recipient's last-known place of abode or business

c) Leaving at or affixing to the leased/mortgaged premises (if serving on a tenant/mortgagor)

s.196 applies to notices *"required or authorised"* to be served by the *Law of Property Act 1925*, or *"required"* to be served by any instrument affecting property. (In the latter case, the absence of the word *"authorised"* has been considered not to make any real difference: *London Borough of Enfield v Devonish* (1997) 29 HLR 691).

- Where *s.23, Landlord and Tenant Act 1927* applies, notices may be served by:

  a) Giving personally to the recipient

  b) Leaving at the recipient's last-known place of abode

  c) Sending by registered or recorded delivery to the recipient's last-known place of abode

s.23 applies to notices served under specific property-related statutes: the *Landlord and Tenant Acts* of *1927*, *1954* and *1988*, also the *Landlord and Tenant (Covenants) Act 1995*.

It has been held in *Galinski v McHugh [1988] 57 P&CR 359* that *s.23* does not preclude service being effected by a method not provided for in that section; it is directory, not mandatory. It is generally considered that the same applies to *s.196*, although in *E.ON v Gilesports [2012] 3 EGLR 23* that proposition was rejected. The point was not argued before the court, however, and the judge gave no authority for that conclusion, so it is considered that the point remains arguable.

Property documents such as leases often expressly incorporate one of these provisions, usually *s.196*.

"*Leaving at*" in these provisions probably means more than putting through a letterbox – the notice should be left with a human being, perhaps a receptionist or security guard.

Limitations to effective service

Two cases decided in relation to *s.196* could have wider application.

In *Blunden v Frogmore Investments [2002] EWCA Civ 573*, a notice was affixed to premises, but the premises had shortly prior to that been seriously damaged by terrorist action, and the security arrangements made it impossible for the tenant to see the notice. It was held that bad faith on the part of the landlord meant that the notice had not been validly served in accordance with *s.196*.

In *Arundel Corporation v Khokher [2003] EWCA Civ 1784*, a tenant sent a notice to the landlord's address stated in the lease – but the tenant's solicitor had been told that the landlord's address had changed, and the tenant was deemed to have that knowledge. The notice had therefore not been sent to the landlord's 'last-known' place of business.

Deemed service provisions

Where notice is sent by a postal method, service is deemed to have taken place on a date determined by rules which differ as between the various methods.

a) Where a notice is sent by ordinary first-class post, *s.7, Interpretation Act 1978* provides that it is deemed to be received in the 'normal course of post' – that is, the next working day after posting. A sender only benefits from *s.7* where the notice is authorised or required by statute to be served by post (so this will apply where notice is served under *s.1139 Companies Act 2006*).

In *Calladine-Smith v Saveorder Ltd [2011] 3 EGLR 55*, it was held:

i.   If the sender can prove the letter has been put in a properly addressed, pre-paid envelope and posted, then the letter is deemed served. It is not enough just to put it in an out-tray.

ii.   If it is necessary to identify the date of service, and if the intended recipient can show on a balance of probabilities that it was delivered late or not at all, that rebuts the presumption of deemed service.

b)   Where a notice is sent by registered or recorded delivery, under *s.196, Law of Property Act 1925*, again it is deemed to be received in the 'normal course of post' – that is, the next working day after posting, unless it is returned undelivered. It was held in *WX Investments v Begg [2002] EWHC 925 (Ch)* that so long as the notice is eventually delivered, the deemed date of service overrides the actual date of delivery.

c)   Where a notice is sent by registered or recorded delivery, under *s.23, Landlord and Tenant Act 1927*, the position is much more advantageous for the sender: service is deemed to have been effected on the date of posting, and even where it is subsequently proved that the notice was never delivered: *CA Webber (Transport) Ltd v Railtrack plc [2003] EWCA Civ 1167*. It is therefore very valuable to take advantage of *s.23*, where this is possible. The Court of Appeal, in *Freetown v Assethold Ltd [2012] EWCA Civ 1657*, has criticised *Webber*, and declined to extend its application to service of notices under the *Party Walls Act 1996*, nevertheless it is still good law as regards service in accordance with *s.23*.

What are Registered post and Recorded delivery?

'Registered post' is defined by *Postal Services Act 2000, s.125* as "*a postal service which provides for the registration of postal packets in connection with their transmission by post and for the payment of compensation for any loss or damage*". The Post Office's 'Special Delivery' service is a registered post service. It guarantees next-day delivery, and if there is no-one there to sign for the item, it will be held for three weeks in a local post office to allow for collection.

'Recorded delivery' is defined by *Postal Services Act 2000, Sched. 8* as a postal service which provides for the delivery of the document by post to be recorded. The Post Office's recorded delivery service is called 'Signed-for'. Delivery by this method can take several days; if there is no-one there to sign for the item, it will be held for only one week in a local post office to allow for collection.

Recorded delivery is cheaper than registered post, though neither is particularly expensive. If either can be used, the best choice is generally registered post (Special Delivery).

Both schemes have a 'track and trace' facility – though the information is only available online for three months from posting, and the Post Office delete their records completely after 12 months.

If there is a risk that the recipient will refuse to sign for the notice, consideration should be given to sending it by normal post as well, despite the deemed service rules. It is always best to be able to prove that the notice has actually been received.

Time limits

Relevant time limits for the statutory notices with which we are concerned will be discussed in the respective chapters. Required length of notice for terminating periodic tenancies has already been discussed in Chapter 2.

As regards exercising a contractual break option, the lease will usually specify a deadline by which notice must be given, although 'rolling breaks' are encountered, under which notice may be given at any time so long as the required length of notice is given. Where there is a deadline, the courts will invariably regard time as being of the essence of the provision: *United Scientific Holdings v Burnley Borough Council [1978] AC 904*. Therefore, if a purported break notice is served after expiry of the deadline, even a day after, the option will not have been validly exercised.

That, of course, makes it crucial to identify the deadline accurately.

Ascertaining the deadline

Ideally, the lease would always specify an actual date as the deadline, so that there could be no room for interpretation or doubt. Often that is not done, and some formula for identifying the deadline is adopted instead; that may be because it is simply not possible to specify an actual date, depending on the circumstances.

However, the absence of an actual date can lead to difficulties: if, for example, a lease provides for a break option operable "*on the third anniversary of the commencement of the term on not less than six months' notice*", it is necessary to identify the term commencement date so as to identify the third anniversary, and also to reach a conclusion as to whether the clause intends "*six clear months*" or not.

The uncertainties potentially present in the first point can be seen in the *Mannai* case. As to the latter point, assuming the third anniversary of the term commencement date to be 25 December, it would be natural to think that the last date for service of notice would be the preceding 25 June. That is only correct, though, if the 'corresponding date rule' applies. This rule was articulated by the House of Lords in *Dodds v Walker [1981] 2 All ER 609*, and the effect is that a notice of so many months expires on the day in the relevant month which bears the same number as the day on which the notice was given. So, the corresponding date to 25 June is 25 December, and a notice given on 25 June to expire on 25 December will therefore have satisfied the requirement for not less than six months' notice.

However, in the commercial landlord and tenant context "*not less than six months*" generally means "*six clear months*", so excluding the day of service and the day of expiry (*Thompson v Stimpson [1960] 3 All ER 500*). On that basis, the latest day for service would be 23 June.

Rather than rely upon matters of interpretation, the safe practical course if there is any doubt is to regard the earliest potential date as the deadline.

If the clause were to require *"six months' notice"*, omitting *"not less than"*, it would seem on the face of it that notice could be served only on one day. That interpretation was rejected as a commercial absurdity in *Hexstone Holdings v AHC Westlink [2010] EWHC 1280 (Ch)*. However, it is possible for a notice to be invalid for having been served too early. In *Biondi v Kirklington and Piccadilly Estates [1947] 2 All ER 59*, the lease contained a call option, entitling the tenant to call for the grant of a new lease by service of notice upon the landlord six months before the expiry of the term. The tenant served the notice in 1911, even though the term did not expire until 1946. The High Court held that the clause should be interpreted as requiring notice to be served within a reasonable time before the expiry of the term.

Identities of sender and recipient

A valid notice must be sent by the correct sender, to the correct recipient.

An example of difficulties arising from inaccurate identification was *Vanquish Properties (UK) Limited Partnership v Brook Street (UK) Ltd [2016] EWHC 1508 (Ch)*, a case relating to a purported break notice served by a landlord. The landlord's interest was leasehold, and it intended to terminate a sub-lease.

The head-lease was granted to a limited partnership acting by its general partner. However, a limited partnership (as with ordinary partnerships) has no legal personality. Therefore, the head-lease could not be vested in it, and the correct analysis was that it was vested in the general partner. It followed that only the general partner was entitled to exercise the break option, and that the purported break notice, served in the name of the limited partnership, was invalid.

Could the notice be saved by applying the *Mannai* test? The court thought not. There was nothing in the letters, notices or surrounding context that would make the mistake clear to the reasonable recipient. Indeed, in the court's view it was far more likely that the reasonable recipient would have appreciated that the legal estate could not be held by the limited partnership (some might think this attributes a high degree of legal sophistication to the reasonable recipient), and would therefore have been puzzled by what the notice meant.

Lay v Ackerman [2004] EWCA Civ 184 is an example of *Mannai* operating to save a notice served by the wrong landlord; the court concluded on the facts that a reasonable recipient of the notice would have understood that it was intended to be served by the correct party. But the very fine factual distinctions made in such cases make it hard to predict which way a particular case might go. Careful investigation of the identity of the parties is therefore essential.

Checking identity

The last rent demand is one useful check on the identity and address of the landlord, though it is not conclusive.

Where the identity of a party needs to be checked, it is often possible to do this by means of a search at the Land Registry, if the party's title is a registered one. However, it is necessary to bear in mind the 'registration gap': in *Brown & Root Technology v Sun Alliance [1997] 1 EGLR 39* it was held that if a registered title is transferred, until the registration has been completed it is only the transferor which can serve or receive notices in relation to that title. That rule was reaffirmed in *Sackville UK Property Select II (GP) No 1 Ltd v Robertson Taylor Insurance Brokers Ltd [2018] EWHC 122 (Ch)*.

So a tenant might have received a notification of change of landlord shortly before it intends to serve a break notice, but notice should still be served on the old landlord, unless and until the registration of the change of landlord has been completed. (In practice, it is often sensible to serve on both the old and the new landlord). Equally, where the lease is registered, there may for example have been an intra-group transfer of the lease shortly before the break notice is to be served, but until the registration is completed, it is the former tenant which must serve the notice.

As regards company details, name and registered office can of course be checked by a search of the Companies Register. It is easy to be caught out by intra-group name-swaps, though, and the key is to focus on the registration number of the company, which will never change. The other useful point to bear in mind is that no two companies can have the same name at the same time.

Take, for example, a situation where

    a)   Shelton Holdings Ltd entered into a lease as landlord,

    b)   there has been no notification of change of landlord, and

    c)   the tenant now intends to serve a break notice.

Although this looks straightforward, there has in fact been an intra-group name-swap, without the tenant ever having been notified. The landlord company is now called Shelton Properties Ltd, while the day-to-day management has been transferred to another group company, now known as Shelton Holdings Ltd, with whom the tenant has been dealing in relation to the property.

When the tenant searches against the name Shelton Holdings Ltd, it should check what that company was called at the date of the lease. The search will reveal that on that date the company was not called Shelton Holdings Ltd, and so it is not the correct company. It will be necessary to search further to find out which company *was* called Shelton Holdings Ltd on that date, which will lead to Shelton Properties Ltd. Once that company has been identified, and its registration number ascertained, it is the company with that number which must be served, whatever it may be called now.

It is now very common practice to incorporate company registration numbers of the parties in leases and other conveyancing documents, to simplify this enquiry.

It is prudent to repeat any searches on the day that the notice is sent out, so as not to be caught out by last-minute changes.

Joint parties

Where there are joint tenants to a lease, all joint tenants must serve the break notice: *Hammersmith and Fulham London Borough Council v Monk [1992] 1 AC 478*. An example of the consequences of failure to do so is provided by *Prudential Assurance Co v Exel [2009] All ER (D) 122 (Sep)*. A lease was held jointly by two group companies, but notice to terminate the lease was sent by only one of them (the other was a dormant company). The result was that the lease was not terminated, and the companies had a continuing rental liability for the rest of the term of the lease.

As noted in Chapter 2, the rule in relation to notice to quit given by a tenant under a periodic tenancy is different: one of joint tenants can give an effective notice (*Hammersmith and Fulham LBC v Monk*).

Preparation and service of a break notice to be given by joint tenants is straightforward: all the joint tenants sign the notice, which is then served on the landlord. By contrast, where notice is to be served upon joint landlords, this may involve some practical issues, the solutions to which are not completely obvious. To take an example:

Four partners in a solicitors' firm were joint tenants of their office premises. Upon relocating, they sub-let the premises. The sub-tenant now wishes to exercise a break option by serving notice on the four partners. There are a number of ways in which this might be attempted:

a) four notices, individually addressed and sent

b) one notice addressed to all, of which four signed originals are sent, one to each

c) one notice addressed to all, but only one signed original sent to the firm's place of business

None of these is necessarily wrong (and one approach might be to do all three simultaneously).

(a) achieves service on each of them, but leaves room for dispute and uncertainty as to when all four have been served, or indeed for one or more of the notices to go astray completely. Plus there may be argument as to whether four documents (which will be different from each other in that they will be addressed to different people) can amount to a single notice; that must ultimately be a matter of construction of the break clause.

(b) is perhaps the safest, though again there is a risk of late delivery, or non-delivery, as regards some of the recipients.

(c) has the advantage that there can be no doubt as to the timing of service, assuming service to have been valid. However, it gives rise to a question as to whether all, or even any, of the individuals can be taken to have been served at all.

Address for service

There are potentially a number of addresses for service of notices. Some of the possibilities and issues have been identified above.

- The lease may specify that notice is to be served at a particular address, in which case notice should be served there if at all possible, regardless of whether notice is simultaneously served at other addresses.

- *s.196 LPA 1925*, or *s.23 LTA 1927* may apply, in which case the applicable address is the recipient's last-known place of abode or business. In the case of service on a tenant under *s.196*, notice may additionally be left at the demised premises.

- In the case of a company, unless this is excluded by a mandatory service provision, notice may also be served at its registered office in accordance with *s.1139* of the *Companies Act 2006* (or under *s.1146*, in the case of an overseas company, at the place specified). Service at a registered office may not in fact bring the notice to the recipient's attention; it may be the office of the company's accountants, or a company formation agent, or some other third party who may not notify the recipient promptly. That does not prevent this being good service, though.

- The recipient may have indicated that notice should be served upon an agent, and sufficient evidence of authority may have been provided. An address for service should have been given as part of that information.

- Where the notice is to be served upon joint parties, then as noted above the judgment may be made that individual documents should be served upon each party, and of course that may involve a number of different addresses.

While the sender may benefit from deemed service provisions, it will always be better to effect service in a way which gives the best chance of the notice coming to the recipient's attention, and so caution may dictate serving to more than one of the possible addresses. Since (see above) it may also be prudent to serve by more than one method, and sometimes on more than one potential recipient, making sure that notice is validly served can involve a lot of paper, and tight organisation.

It is worth noting also that any one of these potential addresses (the only exception being the address registered under the *Companies Act 2006*), may be overseas, and that may mean that more time should be allowed for the practicalities of effecting service.

Summary

A valid notice must:

- Convey the appropriate meaning to implement the contractual or statutory provision under which it is served; in the event of error, the court will consider whether a reasonable recipient would have understood what the notice was intended to achieve, and the notice may be held valid despite the error: *Mannai Investment Co v Eagle Star Life Assurance [1997]*

- Comply with any prescribed formalities

- Contain any information which it is required to contain

- Be served in the prescribed manner

- Be served in accordance with any applicable time limits

- Be served at the correct place

- Be served on the correct recipient

- Be served by the correct sender

CHAPTER FIVE

NOTICE OF NON-CONTINUANCE UNDER SECTION 27(1)

This chapter considers termination of a tenancy by notice under s.27(1) of the 1954 Act.

Our survey of available methods for a tenant to terminate a commercial tenancy now turns to its main focus: termination under the *Landlord and Tenant Act 1954*. As observed previously, the available methods vary as time goes on, depending on the point in the lease term at which termination is to be effected, and the progress which has been made in the procedure under the Act. Our consideration of these methods follows this chronological order, so that we begin with the method which can be employed at the earliest point in the tenancy, namely service of a notice under *s.27(1)*.

s.27(1) provides as follows:

> *"Where the tenant under a tenancy to which this Part of this Act applies, being a tenancy granted for a term of years certain, gives to the immediate landlord, not later than three months before the date on which apart from this Act the tenancy would come to an end by effluxion of time, a notice in writing that the tenant does not desire the tenancy to be continued, section twenty-four of this Act shall not have effect in relation to the tenancy unless the notice is given before the tenant has been in occupation in right of the tenancy for one month."*

In effect, once such a notice has been served, *s.24(1)* is disapplied, so that the tenancy will not be continued beyond its contractual expiry date.

Earliest date for service

It may be noted that the notice could be served at a very early stage. However unlikely such a scenario might be, a tenant might take a lease for a long term such as 50 years, and serve notice under *s.27(1)* immediately after the first month. Once served it could not be retracted, in common with all notices under the Act (with one very limited exception, which is not relevant for present purposes). Any assignee of the lease would have no renewal rights under the Act. The lease would, in effect, be contracted-out as from the date of service.

No substitute for contracting-out

However, this mechanism could not be taken advantage of as a substitute for the usual contracting-out procedure, since the landlord could not compel the tenant to serve the *s.27(1)* notice. Any agreement purporting to require the tenant to do so would fall foul of *s.38(1)* of the Act. That provision states that:

> "*Any agreement relating to a tenancy to which this Part of this Act applies (whether contained in the instrument creating the tenancy or not) shall be void (except as provided by section 38A) in so far as it purports to preclude the tenant from making an application or request under this Part of this Act.*"

The *Law of Property Act 1969* introduced the ability to contract out of the Act, which is now provided for in *s.38A*. Up until then, *s.38(1)* had read as a straightforward prohibition on contracting-out:

> "*Any agreement relating to a tenancy to which this Part of this Act applies (whether contained in the instrument creating the tenancy or not) shall be void in so far as it purports to preclude the tenant from making an application or request under this Part of this Act.*"

It is always worth bearing in mind that, except as regards agreements which comply with *s.38A*, that general prohibition is still present, and will void any agreement which attempts to exclude the operation of Part

II of the Act. An agreement requiring the tenant to serve notice under *s.27(1)* would not fall within *s.38A*.

Latest date for service

The latest date for service of a *s.27(1)* notice is three months before the contractual expiry date. Once that date has passed, the tenant will need to use one of the other methods of termination set out in the following chapters.

Term of years certain

No *s.27(1)* notice can be served in relation to a periodic tenancy, since the provision only applies to tenancies for a term of years certain. The tenant under a periodic tenancy can instead terminate its tenancy by serving notice to quit (see Chapter 2), which remains an effective mode of termination (*s.24(2)*), so that the tenancy is therefore not continued under *s.24(1)*.

This restriction on the application of *s.27(1)*, to tenancies for a term of years certain, provides an instance of the problematic nature of the decision in *London Borough of Newham v Thomas-Van Staden [2008] EWCA Civ 1414*, discussed in Chapter 3. The effect of the decision is that a lease in which the definition of "*the Term*" includes not only the fixed period, but also "*any continuation, extension or holding over*", is not a tenancy for a term of years certain, and cannot therefore be contracted-out. Any purported contracting-out of such a lease will be invalid. There will be a great many leases containing such wording, which the parties will believe to have been contracted-out, but which are not.

How is such a lease to be terminated by the tenant? The effect of serving a *s.27(1)* notice would ordinarily be that the tenancy would not be continued by *s.24(1)*, and would therefore terminate on its contractual expiry date. In the case of leases falling foul of the *Thomas-Van Staden* rule, since the term is not certain, no contractual expiry date can be identified. As suggested in Chapter 3, perhaps the answer is that a periodic tenancy arises after the fixed term, so that service of a notice to quit will effect termination.

Immediate landlord

It should be noted that a *s.27(1)* notice must be served on "*the immediate landlord*". Where a derivative interest such as a sub-lease or sub-underlease comes up for renewal, it is necessary to identify who is the 'landlord' for the purposes of the renewal process: is it the superior landlord, the immediate landlord, or some intermediate landlord? The 'landlord' in such a case is determined in accordance with *s.44*, and is generally referred to as the 'competent landlord'. This enquiry (considered further in Chapter 7) is unnecessary for the purposes of *s.27(1)*, since the consequence of service of a *s.27(1)* notice is that there can be no renewal process. There is therefore no need to identify which superior interest is affected; it is only the immediate landlord who needs to know that the tenancy will be terminating.

Form of notice

There is no prescribed form. Notice is often given by letter, and the wording should track that of the section, for example:

> "*We hereby give you notice, pursuant to s.27(1) of the Landlord and Tenant Act 1954, that our client does not desire its tenancy to be renewed*".

Interaction with s.26

Under *s.26(4)*, the tenant who has served a *s.27(1)* notice cannot then subsequently serve a *s.26* request, or vice versa, which has obvious sense. A tenant cannot have it both ways. The landlord needs to have some certainty as to the tenant's intentions. That said, this rule does not give the landlord complete certainty, since the tenant who has served a *s.26* request is not bound to take a new tenancy, and has the ability to change its mind. The tenant who has served a *s.27(1)* notice, by contrast, is tied to the consequences.

Interaction with s.25

The procedures under the 1954 Act often lead to argument over competing notices. Where the tenant has served a notice which has the effect of terminating its tenancy, the point of the argument will usually be to identify what is the effective termination date, and therefore how much more rent the tenant has to pay.

A landlord might, for example, seek to prolong the tenant's rental liability by serving a 'long' s.25 notice after a s.27(1) notice has been served. If, say, the tenant serves a s.27(1) notice four months before the contractual expiry date, the landlord might respond by immediately serving a s.25 notice expiring at the end of twelve months, with a view to securing another eight months' rent. There is no specific provision in the Act to govern such a situation, but since the effect of the s.27(1) notice is that the continuation tenancy under s.24(1) does not arise, a s.25 notice purporting to terminate it eight months after contractual expiry is an absurdity.

What about if the landlord gets in first? If the landlord serves a twelve-month s.25 notice four months before the contractual expiry date, is the tenant obliged to pay the extra eight months' rent? It is considered that by analogy to *Long Acre Securities Ltd v Electro Acoustic Industries Ltd [1990] 1 EGLR 91*, the tenant can validly serve a s.27(1) notice after the s.25 notice, and the tenancy will come to an end at contractual expiry. (The *Long Acre* case was overruled in *Esselte AB v Pearl Assurance plc [1997] 1 WLR 891*, but not on this aspect, and leading commentators consider that the point is still good law).

Alternative to s.27(1)

There is a further way in which the tenant could bring the tenancy to an end on the contractual expiry date, by simply vacating the premises in accordance with s.27(1A) – this will be dealt with in Chapter 8.

Summary

Tenants under leases which are within the 1954 Act can achieve lease termination at the contractual expiry date, thus avoiding continuation under s.24(1), by serving notice on their immediate landlord under s.27(1).

Notice can be served once the tenant has been in occupation pursuant to the tenancy for one month, but cannot be served any later than three months before the contractual expiry date.

A s.27(1) notice can only be given in relation to a tenancy for a term of years certain, so this procedure is not available in the case of a periodic tenancy.

There is no prescribed form of notice.

A tenant who has served a s.27(1) notice cannot then subsequently serve a s.26 request, or vice versa.

In the event of the landlord serving a s.25 notice with a termination date later than the contractual expiry date, a tenant's s.27(1) notice will nevertheless be effective to terminate the tenancy on the contractual expiry date.

CHAPTER SIX

NOTICE TO TERMINATE
UNDER SECTION 27(2)

This chapter considers termination of a tenancy by notice under s.27(2) of the 1954 Act.

Once into the last three months of the contractual term, the tenant is no longer able to give a non-renewal notice under *s.27(1)*, and there is no other available notice under the Act which could be served so as to prevent the continuation tenancy under *s.24(1)* from coming into effect. However, if the tenant wishes to terminate the continuation tenancy, it can serve a notice under *s.27(2)*, terminating it on not less than three months' notice.

Conditions for application of s.27(2)

s.27(2) provides:

> *"A tenancy granted for a term of years certain which is continuing by virtue of section twenty-four of this Act shall not come to an end by reason only of the tenant ceasing to occupy the property comprised in the tenancy but may be brought to an end on any day by not less than three months' notice in writing given by the tenant to the immediate landlord, whether the notice is given after the date on which apart from this Act the tenancy would have come to an end or before that date, but not before the tenant has been in occupation in right of the tenancy for one month."*

The reference to a tenancy which *"is continuing by virtue of section twenty-four"* appears to suggest that the contractual expiry date must have passed before a *s.27(2)* notice can be given, but clarification is given later in the sub-section that this is not so. What is intended is that the tenancy is continuing under *s.24* at the time the notice takes effect, not when it is served. Since the latest date when a *s.27(1)* notice can be given is three months before the contractual expiry date, and since the required period of notice under *s.27(2)* is at least three months, the intention is clearly that in the last three months of the term the tenant may give a *s.27(2)* notice, which would terminate the tenancy at a point when it could only be "*continuing by virtue of section twenty-four*".

Further, since *s.27(2)* provides that notice may not be served until the tenant has been in occupation under the tenancy for one month, it is clear that notice may be served earlier than the last three months of the term. The tenant has a free choice whether to serve notice under *s.27(1)* or *s.27(2)*, until the last three months.

Should the tenant, after the contractual expiry date, cease to be in business occupation of the property, *s.27(2)* provides that that does not by itself terminate the continuation tenancy. The tenant who wishes to effect termination must serve a *s.27(2)* notice, even though the tenancy has become one to which the Act no longer applies (though see what is said below about service of a *s.27(2)* notice after commencement of court proceedings).

Characteristics of s.27(2) notice

There are the following similarities with a *s.27(1)* notice:

- There is no prescribed form

- It cannot be served until the tenant has been in occupation under the tenancy for one month

- It must be served on the immediate landlord, regardless of who else may be the competent landlord (the issue of identifying the competent landlord is covered in Chapter 7)

- The tenant cannot serve a *s.27(2)* notice if a *s.26* request has been served, or vice versa (*s.26(4)*)

Form of notice

Since there is no prescribed form, a letter will suffice, and it is advisable simply to track the wording of *s.27(2)*. Typically, a *s.27(2)* notice will say something like:

> "*We hereby give you notice under s.27(2) of the Landlord and Tenant Act 1954, bringing our client's tenancy to an end on [date]*".

Interaction with s.25

In Chapter 5 we considered how landlord and tenant may serve competing notices (*s.25* notice served by landlord, *s.27(1)* notice served by tenant), each with a view to manipulating the effective termination date, and therefore the remaining period of rental liability, to their advantage.

Where it is a *s.27(2)* notice which may compete with a *s.25* notice, the position has a little added complexity.

'Long' s.25 notice followed by 'short' s.27(2) notice

The tenant can validly serve a 'short' *s.27(2)* notice following a 'long' *s.25* notice (*Long Acre Securities Ltd v Electro Acoustic Industries Ltd [1990] 1 EGLR 91*), and the earlier termination date will prevail.

'Short' s.27(2) notice followed by 'long' s.25 notice

In Chapter 5 we considered the possibility of a landlord serving a 'long' *s.25* notice in response to a *s.27(1)* notice, and the point was made that since the *s.27(1)* notice has the effect of preventing the continuation tenancy under *s.24(1)* from arising, a subsequent *s.25* notice, purporting to terminate the continuation tenancy at a date later than the contractual expiry date, must be an absurdity. The same cannot be said in relation to *s.27(2)*, the application of which is predicated upon the tenancy being continued under *s.24(1)*. However, if the *s.27(2)* notice was valid when served, it is difficult to see how it can be invalidated by service of a subsequent *s.25* notice, so the earlier termination date originally specified by the tenant should, it is submitted, prevail.

'Long' s.27(2) notice followed by 'short' s.25 notice

Since *s.27(2)* refers to *"not less than three months' notice"*, but does not provide for a maximum notice period, there is in theory no limitation to the length of notice which the tenant might give. A tenant might serve a *s.27(2)* notice expiring ten years hence. Bearing in mind that notice can be given once the tenant has been in occupation by right of the tenancy for one month, a more extreme example might be as follows:

- A grants B a lease of commercial premises for a term of 25 years from 24 June 2021, and B commences business occupation on that date.

- On 2 August 2021, having been in occupation for just over a month, B serves a *s.27(2)* notice on A, purporting to terminate the continuation tenancy on 23 June 2071.

The effect would be to double the length of term. Moreover, under *s.24A(1)*, no application can be made to determine an interim rent during the additional 25 years, since that is only possible where a *s.25* notice or *s.26* request has been served.

Presumably a landlord would respond by serving a *s.25* notice specifying an earlier termination date. It was held in the *Long Acre* case that a tenant can validly serve a *s.27(2)* notice after a *s.25* notice. It is submitted that there is no reason in principle why a landlord could not equally serve a valid *s.25* notice after a *s.27(2)* notice. If both notices were valid, then the earlier termination date specified in the *s.25* notice should be effective. However, the matter has not to date received judicial consideration.

It must be unlikely that any tenant would do something so obviously provocative of litigation as serving a ten-year *s.27(2)* notice, but less extreme examples of 'long' *s.27(2)* notices are certainly encountered. It is not hard to imagine situations in which this might be useful for tenants. For example, a tenant intending to relocate might sign an agreement for lease in relation to new premises, still in the course of construction. If completion of construction, plus the tenant's fit-out, are estimated to take eighteen months, service of an eighteen-month *s.27(2)* notice provides a neat way of terminating the tenant's lease of its present premises at the desired time.

The only other options would be to serve a twelve-month *s.26* request, or wait to see whether the landlord serves a *s.25* notice, of whatever length. It would then be necessary to try to conduct the renewal procedure, specifically the court proceedings, so as to achieve termination at the right time. This would be very uncertain, since it would not be completely within the tenant's control. By contrast, the only uncertainty attendant upon an eighteen-month *s.27(2)* notice would be whether the landlord might respond with a shorter *s.25* notice, and litigate the point just discussed, and there will seldom be sufficient incentive for a landlord to do that.

'Short' s.25 notice followed by 'long' s.27(2) notice

It is perhaps unlikely that a tenant would wish to serve a 'long' *s.27(2)* notice in response to a 'short' *s.25* notice. A tenant that wishes to prolong its tenure of a property has a much more obvious way of achieving that, which is simply to use the 1954 Act for its intended purpose, and apply to court for a new tenancy. Should a tenant choose to do so, however, it is suggested that the same point as made above applies: if the *s.25* notice was valid when served, then it is not invalidated by service of a subsequent *s.27(2)* notice, and so the earlier termination date should be effective.

Apportionment of rent

Before the 2003 reforms to the Act, a *s.27(2)* notice had to specify a termination date which was a quarter day. Now, any termination date can be specified, so long as no less than three months' notice is given. The opportunity was taken, when that change was made, to provide in *s.27(3)* that if any rent was payable by the tenant prior to the termination date, but partly in respect of a period after that date, it should be apportioned. This is the only instance under the 1954 Act in which the tenant is entitled to an apportionment upon termination.

s.27(2) notice following commencement of renewal proceedings

Once an application has been made under Part II of the 1954 Act, whether under *s.24(1)* or *s.29(2)*, and whether made by the tenant or the landlord, *s.64* is engaged. The effect of *s.64* is to rewrite the *s.25* notice or *s.26* request which initiated the renewal process, by substituting a different date of termination. Rather than the date specified in the notice, under *s.64* the tenancy will continue until:

> "*the expiration of the period of three months beginning with the date on which the application is finally disposed of*".

The date of final disposal of the proceedings is:

> "*the earliest date by which the proceedings on the application (including any proceedings on or in consequence of an appeal) have been determined and any time for appealing or further appealing has expired, except that if the application is withdrawn or any appeal is abandoned the reference shall be construed as a reference to the date of the withdrawal or abandonment*"

Since we are concerned with termination by the tenant, we need not consider how *s.64* operates in relation to determination of the application, or any appeal, by the court. For present purposes, the relevant point is that a tenant that has made an application to the court for a new lease may withdraw it by giving a notice of discontinuance, and that will have the effect of terminating the existing tenancy three months after the notice is given. (Consideration will be given to further aspects of termination of the tenancy following the issue of proceedings in Chapter 9).

How this affects the operation of *s.27(2)* is not clear. It is considered by respected commentators that it may not be possible to give notice under *s.27(2)* once the continuation of the tenancy is governed by *s.64*. The question has practical importance, since the provision in *s.27(3)* for apportionment of rent applies where notice is given under *s.27(2)*, but not otherwise.

s.27(2) applies where the tenancy "*is continuing by virtue of section twenty-four*". Once an application has been made to court, engaging *s.64*, it may more accurately be said that the tenancy is continuing by virtue of *s.24* and *s.64*. On one view, that would take the situation outside the scope of *s.27(2)*, though a plausible argument to the contrary would be that it is still *s.24* which continues the tenancy, *s.64* being more of an administrative provision, which alters the period of continuation.

Another issue arises, rather obliquely, from the case of *I & H Caplan v Caplan and Another (No. 2) [1963] 2 All ER 930*. In that case Cross J considered the procedural scheme under the Act with reference to *s.24(3)(a)*.

That provision deals with the position where, at a time after the contractual expiry date,

> "*a tenancy to which this Part of this Act applies ceases to be such a tenancy*",

presumably because the tenant's business occupation has ceased. It provides that the tenancy:

> "*shall not come to an end by reason only of the cesser*",

but enables the landlord to terminate it by serving from three to six months' notice.

Cross J considered that the purpose of this provision was to give the landlord a method of termination when otherwise there would be none. He noted that:

- if, before the cessation of business occupation, a *s.25* notice or *s.26* request had been served, and there had been an application to the court, then *s.64* would apply, and termination of the tenancy would follow from disposal of the proceedings.

- If, on the other hand, the tenancy were to cease to be within Part II before service of either a *s.25* notice or *s.26* request, then the landlord would be unable to serve a *s.25* notice precisely because the tenancy was no longer within the Act. There would be no court application, and *s.64* would never be engaged.

In his view, *s.24(3)(a)* was enacted to enable a landlord to terminate by notice in those limited circumstances, and it followed that no *s.24(3)(a)* notice could be served once an application for a new tenancy had been made.

The Act originally contained no provision equivalent to *s.24(3)(a)* for the benefit of tenants; in the 2003 reforms, though, *s.27(2)* was amended to provide that a tenancy continuing under *s.24* "*shall not come to an end by reason only of the tenant ceasing to occupy the property comprised in the tenancy*". The inference may be drawn that the intention was to equate the position of the tenant with that of the landlord under *s.24(3)(a)*. Thus, the tenant should have the ability to serve a three-month notice, but not where another means of termination is available.

Therefore, it is argued by some, once proceedings have been issued under Part II, neither the landlord (under *s.24(3)(a)*), nor the tenant (under *s.27(2)*), can serve a notice to terminate. Instead, termination will follow from the operation of *s.64*, and a tenant wishing to terminate the tenancy should give notice of discontinuance (or, if still possible, simply go out of occupation prior to lease expiry in reliance on *s.27(1A)*– see Chapter 8).

Another reason for doubting whether a *s.27(2)* notice can be served once proceedings have been issued is that the position would differ depending on whether the process had been begun by a *s.25* notice or a *s.26* request. In the former case, the tenant could serve a *s.27(2)* notice, while in the latter it could not (*s.26(4)*). There is no obvious reason why such a difference should apply.

A practical problem which could follow from service of a *s.27(2)* notice, after issue of proceedings, is that it would be served on the immediate landlord, while it would be the competent landlord (see Chapter 7) which was conducting the renewal process.

In the absence of any authority, the most that can be said is that there is significant doubt over whether a tenant can give a *s.27(2)* notice once an application has been made under Part II, and it may well be that the tenant is restricted in that situation to effecting termination by discontinuing the proceedings, or by going out of occupation prior to the contractual expiry date, if that is still possible. In practice, a pragmatic approach might be to serve a s.27(2) notice as well, and argue later about how much further rent was payable.

Summary

Once into the last three months of the tenancy, no s.27(1) notice can be served, and the tenant may instead give not less than three months' notice to terminate (no maximum length of notice is specified), under s.27(2). A s.27(2) notice may be served earlier than that, however; like a s.27(1) notice, the earliest date at which it may be served is once the tenant has been in occupation pursuant to the tenancy for one month, so for much of the term a s.27(2) notice will be available as an alternative to a s.27(1) notice.

Notice may also be served under s.27(2) after the contractual termination date, though there is doubt as to whether it remains possible once proceedings under Part II have been commenced, at which time the tenant may instead effect termination on three months' notice by giving notice of discontinuance of the proceedings.

There is no prescribed form of s.27(2) notice.

Notice must be served upon the immediate landlord, not the competent landlord (see Chapter 7).

A tenant who has served a s.27(2) notice cannot then subsequently serve a s.26 request, or vice versa.

As regards the interaction with s.25, the position is a little complex, but a broad summary is thought to be that where a tenant has served a s.27(2) notice, and the landlord has served a competing s.25 notice, the earlier termination date will prevail. If there is no competing s.25 notice, it seems that, because no maximum length of notice is specified, a 'long' s.27(2) notice, even very significantly longer than three months, may well be valid and effective.

CHAPTER SEVEN

SECTION 25, SECTION 26, AND COMPETENT LANDLORD

This chapter deals with termination of a tenancy by service of a notice under s.25 or s.26 of the Act. To serve either type of notice, it may be necessary to identify the 'competent landlord', and this is covered also, together with service of notices under s.40 to elicit the information required to identify the competent landlord.

In the last two chapters, we have considered *s.27(1)* and s.27(2) notices, which can be served at the earliest after the tenant has been in occupation pursuant to the tenancy for one month. The next point at which a new type of notice under the Act becomes available is at the other end of the term, 12 months before the contractual expiry date. At that time, the landlord may serve notice under *s.25*, or the tenant may serve a request for a new tenancy under *s.26*.

Unlike the other notices covered in this book, either of these two will initiate the lease renewal procedure. However, they also provide additional routes for termination of the tenancy by the tenant.

As a preliminary matter, it is necessary to identify the 'landlord' for the purposes of the lease renewal procedure, as defined in *s.44*. Any *s.26* request must be served on the landlord so defined, who is also the party entitled to serve a *s.25* notice.

The competent landlord

In the case of a lease which is not subject to any sub-leases, there is no difficulty: the 'landlord' under *s.44* can only be the immediate landlord. It is where the property has been sub-let, so that there are one or more intermediate landlords to choose from as well, that it becomes necessary to provide for identification of the 'landlord' for these purposes. The Act's mechanism for this is a reliable one, and impressively ingenious, though often intricate in its operation.

Say a property is

- let by A to B, then

- sub-let by B to C, then

- sub-underlet by C to D, then

- sub-sub-underlet by D to E.

Identifying the tenant which is entitled to operate the renewal procedure under the Act is simple enough, because there can be no entitlement to renew for a tenant who is not in business occupation. It will always be the occupying tenant at the bottom of the chain which is entitled to renew, in this instance E.

Identifying which of the holders of the superior interests is entitled to operate the renewal procedure as against E requires definition by the Act, however. That person is generally referred to as the "*competent landlord*", a term which is actually used only in the *Sixth Schedule* to the Act, which deals with various complexities which can arise where there are sub-leases.

It is *s.44(1)* which identifies the competent landlord (although it uses the term "*landlord*"). Under that provision, the competent landlord is either

a) a tenant whose tenancy will not come to an end within fourteen months by effluxion of time, or

b) if no party qualifies under (a), the freeholder.

c) A tenant will not qualify under (a) if any notice has been given by virtue of which their tenancy will come to an end within fourteen months.

In our example:

- A, as freeholder, could be competent landlord, but only if none of the inferior leasehold interests qualifies.

- For an inferior leasehold interest to qualify, it must have more than fourteen months left to run when the *s.25* notice or *s.26* request is to be served. Assuming a nominal reversion of only a few days is held by each of B, C and D, none of them could be competent landlord, and it would follow that the competent landlord could only be A. It may be noted at this point that if service of any notice by A, as competent landlord, were to cause loss to any of B, C or D, under *para. 4* of the *Sixth Schedule* A could be required to compensate them.

- The conclusion that A is the competent landlord does depend upon none of B, C or D being in business occupation, having each sub-let the whole of the property. It follows that their tenancy will not be continued under *s.24(1)* beyond its contractual expiry date. The position is less straightforward if one of the sub-lettings, say from D to E, is in respect of part only of the premises, rather than the whole. In that case, D may remain in business occupation of part of the property, and if so its tenancy will automatically continue beyond the contractual expiry date pursuant to *s.24(1)*. It therefore cannot be said that D's tenancy has less than fourteen months to run. Accordingly, D will be E's competent landlord. That position changes if a *s.25* notice is served on D, or if D serves a *s.26* request.

- If D has remained in business occupation of part, and is therefore entitled to renew its tenancy, the question then arises of who might be D's competent landlord. Since (we continue to assume) B and C have only nominal reversions, and are not in business occupation, that must be A.

It can be seen that the identity of the competent landlord may change as time goes on. Assuming, again, that D has sub-let only part of the premises to E, E might quite correctly serve a *s.26* request on D. Alternatively, D might serve a *s.25* notice on E, which would be equally correct. If, however, A were then to serve a *s.25* notice on D, that would change the identity of E's competent landlord to A. A would be bound by the *s.25* notice previously served by D on E, by virtue of *para. 3* of the *Sixth Schedule*.

It will perhaps occur to the reader that this presents E with something of a problem in discovering who its competent landlord is, since it is unlikely to know the duration of all of the superior leasehold interests, nor is it likely to know whether any *s.25* notices or *s.26* requests have been served in relation to them. *s.40* of the Act provides for the landlord and tenant to be able to serve notices on each other to obtain the information needed to identify the occupying tenant and the competent landlord respectively. It is good practice to serve these notices, and may be negligent not to, if there is any doubt.

Notices under s.40

s.40 notices may not be served until two years before the contractual expiry date. In the case of a periodic tenancy, of course, there is no contractual expiry date until the tenancy has been terminated by a contractual notice to quit. This is only an issue for landlords, since a tenant who serves a notice terminating a periodic tenancy may not renew anyway. The landlord will therefore have to serve the notice terminating the periodic tenancy, but can only then serve a *s.40* notice to find out about inferior interests.

Once a *s.40* notice has been served, the recipient must reply within one month. If the recipient gives information in reply, and in the six months following the reply that information subsequently becomes inaccurate (perhaps owing to an assignment or sub-letting), or the recipient discovers that the information was inaccurate in the first place, there is a duty to correct the information within one month of becoming aware of the inaccuracy.

Prior to the 2003 reforms to the Act, there was thought to be no sanction for any failure to respond to a *s.40* notice, or for providing inaccurate information in reply to one. That position has now changed, and an action for damages for breach of statutory duty is available.

It is *s.40(3)* which provides for a tenant to serve notice. The form is prescribed under the *Landlord and Tenant Act 1954 Pt II (Notices) Regulations 2004 (SI 2004/1005)* (the "*Notice Regulations*").

The tenant can serve notice on any landlord, immediate or superior, requiring them to give the information detailed in *s.40(4)*, which is all the information the tenant needs to know in order to identify the competent landlord. If the information provided identifies the holder of a superior interest that the tenant did not previously know about, then of course a further *s.40* notice can be served on that party.

s.40(1) provides for service of notice by a landlord. The form is prescribed by the *Notice Regulations*.

The landlord will very often be in possession of all the relevant information to enable them to serve the appropriate notices down the chain of title. However, it is generally a good idea to check by service of a *s.40(1)* notice. The landlord can serve notice on their tenant or the holder of inferior tenancies, and the notice requires the recipient to provide the information detailed in *s.40(2)*. That information enables the landlord to identify what notices require to be served to become competent landlord as regards the occupational tenant.

It may happen that a *s.40* notice is sent to a recipient, whether landlord or tenant, who has transferred their interest to a third party. In that case, by replying to the sender notifying them of the transfer, and of the transferee's name and address, the recipient is released from the duty to provide information (*s.40A(1)*). Equally, if a party sends a *s.40* notice but then transfers their interest, the recipient will discharge their duty by supplying the information to the sender, so long as unaware of the transfer (*s.40A(3)*); but if the sender has notified them of the transfer, the information must be supplied to the transferee (*s.40A(2)*).

s.25 – Landlord's notice to terminate

The landlord (and for this purpose we are speaking only of the competent landlord, ascertained in accordance with *s.44*), may serve on the tenant holding the occupational interest a notice to terminate their tenancy under *s.25*. The procedure is an alternative to the tenant initiating matters by serving a *s.26* request, and *s.26(4)* prevents administrative confusion by providing that no *s.25* notice can be served once a valid *s.26* request has been served in relation to the tenancy, and vice versa.

While we are generally concerned only with service of notice by tenants, a *s.25* notice presents the tenant with choices. It may decide to accept termination of the tenancy on the date specified by the landlord. In that case, all the tenant need do is omit to make an application to court on or before the landlord's termination date (*s.29A*). If there is a court application made in time, then termination may still be effected by one of the routes covered in Chapter 9. The tenant may, alternatively, opt to terminate the tenancy at an earlier date by serving notice under *s.27(1)* (see Chapter 5) or *s.27(2)* (see Chapter 6), or by going out of occupation prior to the contractual expiry date, if that is earlier than the landlord's termination date (see Chapter 8).

In order to make these choices, the tenant will need to establish whether the landlord's *s.25* notice was valid in the first place, and so we will consider the requirements for an effective *s.25* notice (the general observations on the validity of notices made in Chapter 4 may of course also be relevant).

Has the termination date been calculated correctly?

The notice must specify a termination date, which must be not less than six months and not more than twelve months after the date of service of the notice, and cannot be earlier than the contractual expiry date. This date must often be carefully calculated, since landlords tend to want to specify either the earliest or latest possible termination date, and the date of service will depend upon the method of service adopted (see Chapter 4).

In the case of a periodic tenancy, there is no contractual expiry date as such, since the tenancy will perpetually renew at the end of each period automatically, unless and until brought to an end by service of a notice. To operate the procedure under the Act, the landlord must therefore 'generate' a contractual expiry date by giving a contractual notice to terminate the periodic tenancy. The length of notice required will depend on the terms of the tenancy, or more often on the common law rules, in the absence of express provision in the tenancy agreement.

As considered in Chapter 2, the common law rule is that the landlord must give at least one full period's notice, expiring on the final day of a period; in the case of an annual periodic tenancy, though, the minimum period is six months, not one year. Since most commercial periodic tenancies are annual ones, this is the usual position. Hence, if a client gives instructions on 1 November to terminate a periodic tenancy which runs annually from 1 October, the earliest expiry date which could be specified would be the following 1 October, eleven months away. That is because a six-month notice would not expire on the final day of a period.

It is important to appreciate that the notice to terminate would only have the effect of terminating the periodic tenancy as a matter of contract. Upon expiry of the notice the statutory continuation tenancy arises under s.24, and to terminate the tenancy under the Act the landlord would still have to serve a s.25 notice; of course, the earliest termination date which could be specified in the s.25 notice would be the expiry date of the contractual notice. For convenience, landlords may simply serve a s.25 notice, which serves as a contractual notice too – the validity of this 'double duty' follows from the wording of s.25(3), and was upheld in *Jones v Daniels & Davidson (Holdings) [1981] CLY 1513*.

'Double duty' is only possible where the length of notice required under the terms of the tenancy is between six and twelve months, since that is the requirement which applies to the s.25 notice. If, for example, the tenancy required eighteen months' notice, the landlord would have to serve the contractual notice, and then wait until within twelve months of the expiry date to serve a s.25 notice.

The same considerations apply to the exercise of a landlord's right to break, but there is a specific provision in s.25(3)(b) in relation to tenancies requiring notice of more than six months, effectively extending the maximum length of notice under s.25 from 12 months to the required contractual length of notice plus six months.

Does the notice contain the required content?

The *Notice Regulations* prescribe the form of notice. The prescribed form requires that the landlord identify the premises to which it relates; usually, this is unproblematic, and the description of the premises in the existing lease is adopted. It should be noted that the notice must relate to the whole of the premises comprised in the lease, even though there may be a sub-tenant of part which is entitled to renew its sub-lease: *Southport Old Links v Naylor [1985] 1 EGLR 66*. Also, if the tenant has more than one tenancy of several properties from the same landlord, a notice which relates to more than one tenancy will be valid (*Tropis Shipping Ltd v Ibex Properties Ltd [1967] EGD 433*), so long as the contractual expiry dates of the various tenancies are such as to make it possible to combine notices in this way while still complying with *s.25*. It might be anticipated that a multi-tenancy notice would unnecessarily complicate procedures.

There are, to be accurate, two prescribed forms of *s.25* notice: one to be used where the landlord does not oppose the grant of a new tenancy, and a different one for use where it does. A "*form to substantially the like effect*" may be used instead of the prescribed form, but of course it is always preferable to use the prescribed form, obtainable via an online forms package or from law stationers. It has been held that minor omissions or errors do not invalidate a notice, so long as the tenant is given the information it needs in order to be able to determine its course of action: *Barclays Bank Ltd v Ascott [1961] 1 WLR 717*.

The notice must state:

- Whether or not the landlord opposes the grant of a new tenancy (*s.25(6)*);

- If it opposes the grant of a new tenancy, the grounds of opposition on which it will rely (*s.25(7)*); and

- If it does not oppose a new tenancy, its proposals in relation to the new tenancy (*s.25(8)*), specifically:

- o the property to be comprised in the new tenancy;

- o the rent to be payable under the new tenancy; and

- o the other terms of the new tenancy.

As regards opposition to the grant of a new tenancy, a landlord can only rely upon grounds stated in the s.25 notice (s.30(1)), so the landlord should have thought carefully when serving notice about which if any grounds to specify. It should be noted that although the landlord will have to prove any statutory ground of opposition at trial, that ground does not generally have to be substantiated as at the date of the notice (*Betty's Cafes Ltd v Phillips Furnishing Stores Ltd [1959] AC 20*). For example, a landlord who intends to offer suitable alternative accommodation to the tenant need not have actually made the offer by the time the notice is served. All that the notice does is notify the tenant of the case it will have to meet at trial.

It is generally thought that a landlord must have an honest belief in the grounds specified: *Stradbroke v Mitchell [1991] 1 EGLR 1*, and that a notice may be invalidated if lack of such a belief can be proved.

Are the proposed terms adequately set out?

As to the terms to be specified in relation to the new tenancy, it is arguable by analogy with *Viscount Chelsea v Morris [1999] 1 EGLR 59* that the rent specified in the notice must be a realistic one, and that if it is not the notice may be invalidated. This is an issue upon which clients or their surveyors sometimes need reassurance, because it is not uncommon for them to be in a position where they are confident that the evidence supports a certain rental value at the date when the notice is being prepared, but they are optimistic that by the date of the trial, perhaps because of market movement generally, or perhaps because of pending transactions to be completed on comparable properties, they may be able to justify a higher rental. Is it safe to specify the anticipated higher rental value, or does that run the risk of invalidating the notice? The difference in the *Viscount Chelsea* case was a very significant one (between £100 and £100,000) and respected commentators take the view that the case cannot be applied by analogy to 1954 Act renewals.

It is an open question how much detail is required in specifying 'other terms', and whether a notice containing insufficient detail might be invalid. The question remains open because no tenant has yet challenged the validity of a notice on this basis in a decided case. In practice landlords often state proposals in the form of a very brief summary, such as:

- A term of 15 years, with provision for upward-only rent review every five years

- On a full repairing and insuring basis

- Including provision for payment by the tenant of a service charge

- And otherwise upon terms appropriate to a modern commercial letting, as contained in the landlord's current standard form of lease.

While the proposed terms may very likely be disputed, it is rare for there to be argument over the validity of the notice based on lack of detail.

Is there any potential for the notice to be withdrawn?

Generally speaking, notices under the 1954 Act cannot be withdrawn; there is, however, a very limited provision for service of a *s.25* notice to be withdrawn, in circumstances which are best explained by an illustrative example.

- Say a commercial property is let by A to B, and then half of it is sub-let by B to C. As appears from the discussion earlier in this chapter, B is C's competent landlord so long as it remains in business occupation of the part of the premises which has not been sub-let, and so long as no *s.25* notice or *s.26* request has been served in relation to its tenancy.

- Twelve months before the contractual expiry of C's sub-lease, B serves a *s.25* notice on C, indicating that grant of a new tenancy will not be opposed. B promptly sends a copy of this notice to A, as required by *para. 7* of the *Sixth Schedule* to the Act. A had intended to obtain possession from B and C in order to redevelop the property, but it can only do so following service on B and C of *s.25* notices specifying the appropriate ground of opposition. Since a valid *s.25* notice has been served on C, specifying no ground of opposition, this presents A with a difficulty.

- A's difficulty can be overcome, under *para. 6* of the *Sixth Schedule*. Where a superior landlord becomes competent landlord after a *s.25* notice has been served, the new competent landlord can withdraw the notice within two months of it being served. Thus, A can serve on B an opposing *s.25* notice, which means that it becomes C's competent landlord; it can then take advantage of *para. 6* by withdrawing the notice served on C by B, and serving its own instead, this time specifying the ground of opposition.

This is the only instance in the Act of an ability to withdraw a notice.

No counter-notice required

Prior to 2004, a tenant in receipt of a *s.25* notice had two months in which to serve a counternotice, stating whether it was prepared to give up possession of the premises upon expiry of the notice, and stating also any counter-proposals for the terms of the new lease. The tenant who failed to serve counternotice within the time limit lost its right to a new lease, and the tenancy would therefore come to an end upon expiry of the *s.25* notice. While there was some benefit to the landlord in being given a formal indication of the tenant's intentions, in practice a tenant would almost always make its plans sufficiently clear in less formal responses to the notice, and this requirement for a counternotice simply served as a trap for unwary tenants. It was abolished in the 2003 reforms.

s.26 – Tenant's request for new tenancy

The other route to initiating the renewal process is for a tenant to serve a request for a new tenancy under *s.26* of the Act. As previously noted, *s.26(4)* provides that no *s.26* request can be served once a valid *s.25* notice has been served in relation to the tenancy, and vice versa.

Service of the request does not, though, commit the tenant to a new tenancy. By omitting to make a court application prior to the date specified in the request, the tenant can effect termination at that date (*s.26(5)* and *s.29A*). If there is a court application made in time, then termination may still be effected by one of the routes covered in Chapter 9. A *s.26* request therefore represents a method of terminating the tenancy while, on the face of it, indicating that the tenant wishes to remain in the property.

The request must be served on the competent landlord, and of course it is only a tenant with an occupational interest which is entitled to renew, and therefore to serve a *s.26* request. However, not all tenants can serve one: the section restricts the availability of the procedure so that it cannot be used by tenants under a periodic tenancy, or tenants with a fixed term for a year or less.

Like a *s.25* notice, it must also specify a date, though in the case of a *s.26* request it is not a termination date but a commencement date: that is, the date on which the new tenancy is requested to commence. Again, it must be not less than six months and not more than twelve months after the date of service of the notice, and cannot be earlier than the contractual expiry date.

As in the case of a *s.25* notice, the *Notice Regulations* prescribe the form of the *s.26* request, and again a *"form to substantially the like effect"* may be used instead of the prescribed form.

The required information is similar to that required to be included in a *s.25* notice, though of course there is no mention of opposition to a new tenancy. Under *s.26(3)* the request must state the tenant's proposals in relation to the new tenancy, specifically:

- the property to be comprised in the new tenancy;

- the rent to be payable under the new tenancy; and

- the other terms of the new tenancy.

It was held in *Sun Life Assurance Plc v Thales Tracs Ltd [2001] 1 WLR 1562* that there is nothing in the Act to indicate any required state of mind or intention on the tenant's part when serving the *s.26* request, and the proposals need not be genuine proposals. A tenant may therefore have already negotiated a new lease of alternative premises, but still serve a valid *s.26* request, despite having no intention to renew its lease, for example in order to secure an entitlement to statutory compensation under the 1954 Act.

There is no provision in the Act for a *s.26* request to be withdrawn.

The requirement for a counternotice to be served within two months, abolished from 2004 in relation to *s.25* notices, has been retained in relation to *s.26* requests. The landlord who has received a *s.26* request has two months in which to serve a counternotice under *s.26(6)*. The purpose of this is that the landlord is required to commit itself at this initial stage, as it would if serving a *s.25* notice, as to whether it intends to oppose the grant of a new tenancy, and if so on what grounds. As in the case of a *s.25* notice, the landlord can only rely upon grounds stated in this counternotice (*s.30(1)*).

Summary

Service of either a s.26 request or a s.25 notice opens up options for the tenant to terminate its current tenancy, either by failing to make a court application in time, or if one is made in time, by adopting one of the termination methods covered in Chapter 9.

Where one or more sub-leases exist, so that there is not only a freeholder but also at least one intermediate landlord, it is necessary to identify the 'competent landlord' for the purposes of the renewal process. The competent landlord is either:

a) a tenant whose tenancy will not come to an end within fourteen months by effluxion of time, or

b) if no party qualifies under (a), the freeholder.

c) A tenant will not qualify under (a) if any notice has been given by virtue of which their tenancy will come to an end within fourteen months.

Tenants can serve notice under s.40, in the last two years of the term, to elicit the information required to identify who is the competent landlord.

A tenant will need to consider whether the landlord has served a valid s.25 notice, and/or what are the requirements for a valid s.26 request.

CHAPTER EIGHT

TERMINATION BY GOING OUT OF OCCUPATION

This chapter deals with termination of the tenancy by going out of occupation prior to contractual expiry, pursuant to s.27(1A).

We remarked in Chapter 1 on the central importance of business occupation to the scheme of protection under the Act. The fact that a tenant can, in effect, disapply the Act so as to terminate its tenancy, simply by going out of occupation, is the clearest possible demonstration of that.

This mechanism for termination first emerged in caselaw, though in the 2003 reforms to the Act a new *s.27(1A)* was inserted, to confirm the position as established by the courts.

Pre-2003 caselaw

Benedictus v Jalaram [1989] 1 EGLR 251

This case proceeded upon the tacit assumption that the existing tenancy would not continue under *s.24(1)* unless the tenants had remained in occupation at the contractual expiry date. The facts are unusual, the relevant history being as follows:

25 March 1982 – This was the contractual expiry date.

11 February 1983 – The tenant served a *s.26* request.

15 June 1983 – The tenant issued its court application for a new tenancy, indicating that it was in occupation of the whole of the premises.

23 April 1987 – The tenant wrote to the landlord stating that it was not in occupation, and therefore not entitled to renew.

30 June 1987 – The court dismissed the application for a new tenancy. The landlord's application for interim rent survived.

29 September 1987 – The tenant filed an answer to the interim rent application, stating that it had not been in occupation at any time after the lease expiry on 25 March 1982, and that there was therefore no jurisdiction to determine interim rent.

The answer was struck out, hence there was no evidence as to whether they had in fact been in occupation at lease expiry. The Court of Appeal upheld the strike-out. The tenant was not entitled to 'approbate and reprobate', by making an application based upon occupation, and then denying occupation and asserting no entitlement to renew, so as to avoid an interim rent determination. The answer to the interim rent application was an abuse of process.

It was unnecessary to the decision for the court to consider whether being out of occupation at lease expiry would prevent continuation of the tenancy, but that conclusion is implicit in the parties' positions and the Court's judgments.

Esselte AB v Pearl Assurance plc [1997] 1 EGLR 73

This is the case which established the effect of the tenant going out of occupation. The chronology is as follows:

6 December 1992 – The tenant went out of occupation

16 January 1993 – The tenant gave notice under *s.27(2)*, expiring on 24 June 1993

14 February 1993 – This was the contractual expiry date

The landlord claimed rent for the period up to expiry of the *s.27(2)* notices, on 24 June 1993, while the tenant paid only up to the contractual expiry date on 14 February 1993.

The Court of Appeal held, referring to the wording of *s.24(1)*, that:

"The stipulation that 'a tenancy to which this Part of this Act applies shall not come to an end unless terminated in accordance with the provisions of this Act' has no effect on a tenancy to which the Act does not apply at the time of its termination. "

It followed that the tenancy determined on its contractual expiry date and was not continued under *s.24*, and the landlord was not entitled to the additional rent which it claimed.

The case received a significant amount of adverse comment. From a landlord's point of view, all other mechanisms of termination under the Act (*s.25, s.26, s.27(1), s.27(2), s.64*) give the landlord at least three months' notice of termination. This allows time to assess the state of repair of the property, decide upon future strategy, prepare letting particulars and conduct viewings, with a view to the resumption of income at the earliest opportunity. The impact of *Esselte* is that a tenant might vacate a property at the last minute, leaving the landlord completely unprepared for lease termination.

Single Horse Properties Ltd v Surrey County Council [2002] EWCA Civ 367

This decision confirmed *Esselte*, and applied it in circumstances where the tenant had made an application for a new tenancy, so that the applicability of *s.64* was an issue. Again, the chronology is helpful:

3 December 1999 – The landlord served a *s.25* notice terminating the tenancy on 24 June 2000 (the contractual expiry date).

21 March 2000 – The tenant issued its court application for a new tenancy

13 June 2000 – The tenant vacated the property, notifying the landlord and returning the keys a few days afterwards

24 June 2000 – This was the contractual expiry date, and also the termination date specified in the landlord's *s.25* notice.

103

22 August 2000 – The court struck out the application for a new tenancy, and made the further order sought by the landlord that the tenant should pay rent for a further three months from the date of the order, that is, up to 22 November 2000. That order clearly rested upon the effect of *s.64*: to continue the tenancy, once a court application has been made, for three months from final disposal of the proceedings.

It was held in the Court of Appeal that *s.64* could not apply. On a correct interpretation, it applies where a notice has been served whose effect, had it not been for *s.64*, would have been to terminate the tenancy at a date earlier than that provided for in *s.64*. Applying *Esselte* to the facts of this case, the tenancy had not been continued by *s.24(1)*, and had therefore come to an end at its contractual expiry date. It followed that the landlord's *s.25* notice, purporting to terminate the tenancy at contractual expiry, had been of no effect, and *s.64* could have no application.

As in *Esselte*, the landlord was not entitled to rent beyond the contractual expiry date, for a period during which there had been no tenancy and the tenant had not been in occupation.

A warning note was sounded in the judgment of Arden LJ, however:

> "If ... the landlord is led by the tenant's conduct to believe that the tenant continues in occupation there is a risk that, in the events which happened, as in Benedictus v Jalaram Ltd [1989] 1 EGLR 251, the tenant will be held to have estopped himself from denying that he was in occupation at the term date and be liable for continuing rent accordingly."

Confirmatory legislation – s.27(1A)

While there may have been some discontent among landlords and their advisers as to the effect of *Esselte* and *Single Horse*, the 2003 reforms included the insertion of a new, confirmatory *s.27(1A)*:

> "Section 24 of this Act shall not have effect in relation to a tenancy for a term of years certain where the tenant is not in occupation of the

property comprised in the tenancy at the time when, apart from this Act, the tenancy would come to an end by effluxion of time."

The effect is that so long as the tenant has ceased to occupy the holding on the contractual expiry date, the tenancy terminates on that date. No notice need be served to terminate the tenancy in this way. Moreover, any prior notice or court application is irrelevant. A tenant may have served a *s.26* request, issued and served a court application, and complied with all case management directions; indeed, the case may be two weeks away from trial, but so long as the tenant's subsequent vacation of the property happens on or before the contractual expiry date, the tenancy will terminate then. No doubt such a history would affect what order the court might make as to the costs of the proceedings, but the termination would be effective.

For the tenant who secures other premises late in the day, this provides a useful escape route, since the alternative would be to serve a *s.27(2)* notice and incur a further three months' rental liability.

It would be a sanguine tenant, though, who relied upon *s.27(1A)* for its termination strategy, counting upon vacating before the contractual expiry date so as to keep its options open until the last minute. Cases concerning the issue of whether a tenant has complied with an obligation to give vacant possession, as a condition of exercising a break option, demonstrate how a tenant may be considered to have remained in occupation by reason of having left goods at the property (e.g. *Secretary of State for Communities and Local Government v South Essex College of Further and Higher Education [2016] PLSCS 249 (Central London County Court, 28 July 2016)*). Another pitfall might be having workmen remaining in the property after lease expiry, even if only for a couple of days, in order to finish off works of repair or decoration (e.g. *NYK Logistics (UK) Limited v Ibrend Estates BV [2011] EWCA Civ 683*).

It is usually preferable to serve the appropriate statutory notice, if time allows, to give certainty. It may be noted that in *Esselte* the tenant had served notices under *s.27(2)*, which was prudent, but because it had given up occupation prior to contractual expiry, it avoided paying additional rent up to the later date when the notices expired.

Summary

Under s.27(1A) so long as the tenant has ceased to occupy the holding on the contractual expiry date, the tenancy terminates on that date.

No notice need be served to terminate the tenancy in this way.

Moreover, any prior notice or court application is irrelevant. Because s.24 does not apply, neither does s.64.

The tenant should notify the landlord when it goes out of occupation, and avoid leading the landlord to believe that it remains in occupation; otherwise, it runs a risk of being estopped from denying that it was out of occupation at the contractual expiry.

It may be prudent to serve notice under s.27(1) or (2) as well as going out of occupation, to put the matter beyond doubt.

CHAPTER NINE

TERMINATION AFTER THE ISSUE OF PROCEEDINGS

This chapter considers the means by which a tenant can effect termination of its tenancy following the issue of proceedings under Part II of the 1954 Act.

In Chapter 6, we discussed the significant doubt as to whether a tenant can validly serve a *s.27(2)* notice to terminate its tenancy, once court proceedings have been issued under Part II of the Act. At that stage, *s.64* operates to extend the interim continuation of the tenancy. *s.64(1)* provides:

> "*In any case where—*
>
> a) *a notice to terminate a tenancy has been given under … Part II of this Act or a request for a new tenancy has been made under Part II thereof, and*
>
> b) *an application to the court has been made under … section 24(1) or 29(2) of this Act, as the case may be, and*
>
> c) *apart from this section the effect of the notice or request would be to terminate the tenancy before the expiration of the period of three months beginning with the date on which the application is finally disposed of,*
>
> *the effect of the notice or request shall be to terminate the tenancy at the expiration of the said period of three months and not at any other time.*"

While this means that a tenant that has applied for a new tenancy under *s.24(1)* can terminate the existing tenancy by discontinuing the proceedings, as stated in Chapter 6, that is not the only means by which proceedings can be *"finally disposed of"*. At this stage, to achieve termination of the tenancy under *s.64*, it is not principally the complexities of the 1954 Act, but the courts' procedures under the *Civil Procedure Rules* which must be successfully navigated.

Some clarification as to what is meant by *"finally disposed of"* is offered by *s.64(2)*:

> *"The reference in paragraph (c) of subsection (1) of this section to the date on which an application is finally disposed of shall be construed as a reference to the earliest date by which the proceedings on the application (including any proceedings on or in consequence of an appeal) have been determined and any time for appealing or further appealing has expired, except that if the application is withdrawn or any appeal is abandoned the reference shall be construed as a reference to the date of the withdrawal or abandonment."*

Proceedings may be disposed of by court order, whether a strike-out or dismissal of an application under *s.24(1)*, or determination in the landlord's favour of an application under *s.29(2)*. If so, it is not the date of the court's order which is the 'final disposal', but the end of the 21-day period within which an appeal may be lodged (*Civil Procedure Rules, r.52.4*). If there is no appeal, the tenancy will therefore terminate three months and 21 days after the order. If an appeal is lodged, the tenancy will terminate three months after the determination of the appeal.

However, we are not concerned with termination as a result of the court's decision, but with how the tenant's actions can bring termination about. The available options differ according to whether proceedings have been issued by the landlord or by the tenant.

s.27(2) notice

As already discussed, it may well be that service of a *s.27(2)* notice is not possible once *s.64* is engaged. However, since there is no decided case dealing with the point, a tenant might serve a *s.27(2)* notice anyway, on the chance that it could be valid. The tenant will then have the opportunity at least to argue about what termination date applies, and also as to whether it benefits from a rent apportionment under *s.27(3)*.

In view of the doubt, though, it would be rash to rely upon a *s.27(2)* notice, and the tenant would no doubt wish to take whatever other action might be available to it as well.

Proceedings issued by tenant – failure to serve

Once proceedings are issued, the claim form must be served within four months (*Civil Procedure Rules, r.7.5*). If service is not effected within that time limit, then the claim form is no longer valid, and cannot be proceeded upon. Might a tenant therefore, having issued proceedings but then decided to terminate the tenancy, simply omit to serve the claim form?

It is unclear whether this would mean that the application had been *"finally disposed of"*. While no action could be taken upon it, it would not have been formally struck out or dismissed, and the wording of *s.64(2)*, referring to proceedings having *"been determined"*, may require that there has been some decision or administrative action on the part of the court.

In view of the uncertainty, a tenant in that position would usually do better to serve the claim form, swiftly followed by a notice of discontinuance.

Proceedings issued by tenant – discontinuance

Under *s.64(2)*, final disposal of proceedings may take place by the application being *"withdrawn"*. In the *Civil Procedure Rules*, the process of withdrawing a claim is referred to as 'discontinuance' (*per* Lewison LJ in *Spicer v Tuli [2012] EWCA Civ 845 "Under the CPR an action cannot be withdrawn. It may either be discontinued under CPR Part 38 or it may be dismissed."*)

Having made the application it is open to the tenant to discontinue it at any time, under *Civil Procedure Rules, r.38.2(1)*. Permission of the court, or consent of specified third parties, may be required in circumstances set out in *r.38.2(2)*, but those circumstances are unlikely to apply to lease renewal proceedings.

Discontinuance is effected by filing at court a notice of discontinuance on Form N279, and serving copies of it on all other parties to the action. The form filed at court must state that it has been so served, and a statement to that effect appears on the standard Form N279 published by HM Courts & Tribunals Service.

Discontinuance takes effect on the day that a copy of the notice is served on the defendant, and the tenancy will terminate three months after that, under *s.64*. This therefore provides a method of termination roughly equivalent to the service of a *s.27(2)* notice. There are two differences, which may be significant, depending on the circumstances:

- As discussed in Chapter 6, service of a *s.27(2)* notice, terminating the tenancy at any time other than the end of a rental period, gives rise to an apportionment of rent under *s.27(3)*. If notice of discontinuance is served so as to terminate the tenancy under *s.64*, there is no apportionment. With rent generally being payable in advance, this is likely to be to the tenant's disadvantage.

- Under *Civil Procedure Rules r.38.6*, a claimant who discontinues will usually be required to pay the defendant's costs of the proceedings. If there has been substantial progress towards trial, and compliance with case management directions, this may be a significant sum. One matter to be aware of is that this may include costs of drafting and negotiating the lease, as well as litigation costs, since there may well have been case management directions requiring submission of a lease, and comments by both parties. Even if this has not been the subject of any direction of the court, it is highly arguable that these are recoverable as costs of settlement negotiations; after all, the whole object of lease renewal proceedings is a new lease.

Proceedings issued by landlord – requirement to serve

A landlord that suspected its tenant intended imminently to take action to terminate its tenancy might issue proceedings (whether under *s.24(1)* or *s.29(2)* would not really matter) and delay service to the last moment, so as to prolong the tenant's rental liability. It would not be until the proceedings had been served that the tenant would be in a position to take any of the actions outlined below to effect termination of the tenancy.

The remedy for the tenant in that situation is contained in *Civil Procedure Rules r.7.7*. Under that provision the defendant to a claim can give notice to the claimant requiring them to serve the claim form, or discontinue the claim, within a specified period (not less than 14 days). If the claimant does not comply, the court may, on the claimant's application, make any order it thinks just, including dismissal of the claim.

Proceedings issued by landlord – discontinuance

Where it is the landlord that has issued proceedings for a new tenancy under *s.24(1)*, it is provided by *s.24(2C)* that it cannot discontinue them without the tenant's consent (and the tenant's consent should be supplied to the court together with the landlord's Form N279 in such a case).

The reason for this requirement is that otherwise the landlord might circumvent security of tenure by issuing and immediately discontinuing renewal proceedings. The same restriction applies, for the same reason, if the landlord issues an application for determination of the tenancy under *s.29(2)*, by virtue of equivalent provision in *s.29(6)*.

Clearly, if the tenant wishes to terminate the tenancy, and the landlord is obliging enough to request consent to discontinuance, the tenant should consent.

It follows from the fact that the application was made by the landlord that it cannot be discontinued by the tenant. This was confirmed, if confirmation were necessary, in *NM Pensions Ltd v Lloyds TSB Bank plc [2009] PLSCS 297*. However, the tenant is not left without a means of termination, though the mechanism varies as between landlord's applications under *s.24(1)* and those made under *s.29(2)*.

Proceedings issued by landlord under s.24(1)

Where the landlord's application was made under *s.24(1)*, the tenant may inform the court under *s.29(5)* that it does not want a new tenancy, and this operates in a similar way to a notice of discontinuance.

There is no prescribed form for this, and it will usually be done by a simple letter to the court. The letter will identify the proceedings in the usual manner, but then need only say something like:

> "*We hereby inform you, pursuant to s.29(5) of the Landlord and Tenant Act 1954, that the defendant does not want a new tenancy of the premises which are the subject of these proceedings*".

It was held in *NM Pensions* that where a tenant gives the court a notification under *s.29(5)*, the court has no discretion, but must dismiss the landlord's application; indeed it has a positive statutory obligation to dismiss it forthwith, and no further application by either party is required. The judge's order should include a declaration that the dismissal takes effect from the date when the tenant's notification is received by the court.

It may be helpful to remind the court of this guidance in the letter.

Under *s.64*, the tenancy will terminate three months and 21 days after the date of the order dismissing the landlord's claim.

As to costs, the notification under *s.29(5)* is treated as a discontinuance by the tenant for this purpose, so that it will usually be required to pay the landlord's costs of the proceedings (*Lay v Drexler [2007] EWCA Civ 464*).

Proceedings issued by landlord under s.29(2)

Proceedings issued under *s.29(2)* present the tenant with more of a problem, since the *s.29(5)* notification procedure applies only to landlord's applications made under *s.24(1)*. On the basis that no *s.27(2)* notice can be served, there is no statutory mechanism by which the tenant can effect termination in these circumstances, other than to ensure, for the purposes of *s.64*, that the landlord's application is determined as soon as possible. Termination of the tenancy is precisely what the landlord is seeking under *s.29(2)*, so the key for the tenant is not to oppose that.

If the tenant's decision to bring its tenancy to an end is taken before any defence has been served to the landlord's *s.29(2)* claim, then it may notify the landlord and the court that it does not intend to defend the claim or seek a new tenancy, and omit to file a defence. The landlord's claim will be brought under *Part 7* of the *Civil Procedure Rules* (see *Practice Direction 56, para. 56.2.1A*) and so judgment in default is not ruled out, as it is in relation to claims where the landlord does not oppose the grant of a new tenancy, which are brought under *Part 8*. The landlord may be left to enter judgment, or the tenant may take the initiative by inviting the landlord to join in a consent order terminating the existing tenancy, or failing that, inviting the court to make an order for termination.

If the decision to terminate was taken after service of a defence, the tenant would need to amend its defence to withdraw opposition to the landlord's claim, and invite the court to make an order for termination.

The date of termination would be either the date specified in the *s.25* notice or *s.26* request or, if later, three months and 21 days after the date of the judgment or court order (the 21-day appeal period should be added even in the case of a consent order, as the Court of Appeal indicated in *DMR v IX [2020] EWCA Civ 377* that an appeal from a consent order would be possible, though very rarely).

s.27(1A)

Proceedings are often issued quite close to the deadline for doing so, which is the date specified in the *s.25* notice or *s.26* request. That date cannot, of course, be any earlier than the contractual expiry date, and quite often a date after contractual expiry will have been specified. This means that by the time proceedings have been issued and served, it is very often the case that contractual expiry is imminent, or already in the past.

It is seldom, therefore, following issue of proceedings, that the tenant finds itself in a position to take advantage of *s.27(1A)*, as discussed in the last chapter. If circumstances do permit, though, and regardless of whether the proceedings were issued under *s.24(1)* or *s.29(2)*, or whether they were issued by tenant or landlord, simply going out of occupation on or before the contractual expiry date provides a simple and reliable means of terminating the tenancy, which will be effective despite *s.64* (*Single Horse Properties Ltd v Surrey County Council [2002] EWCA Civ 367*). It has the added advantage that the termination is immediate, so that rental liability is not prolonged by any notice period.

s.36(2)

A provision of the Act which is very seldom implemented, *s.36(2)* provides tenants with a means to terminate their existing tenancy even after the court has made an order for a new tenancy. Within 14 days of the order being made, the tenant can apply to the court for revocation of the order, and the court must oblige; it has no discretion to refuse revocation.

The existing tenancy will then continue for at least as long as it would otherwise have continued under *s.24* and *s.64*, subject to:

a) the parties agreeing some longer period, or

b) the court determining that it should continue for a longer period, if that is necessary to give the landlord a reasonable opportunity for re-letting.

While *s.36(3)* provides that any costs award made when the order for the new tenancy was granted should be unaffected by revocation under *s.36(2)*, there is a very big 'but':

> *"but the court may, if it thinks fit, revoke or vary any such provision"*.

It must be likely that the court will generally think fit to re-address the issue of costs. In *Nihad v Chain [1956] EGD 234 CC*, for example, the original order that the tenant should pay one-third of the landlord's costs was replaced by an order that the tenant should pay all of the costs.

The likely adverse costs consequences, plus the potential for the continuation of the existing tenancy to be prolonged significantly, make revocation under *s.36(2)* very much a last resort.

Summary

Where proceedings have been issued under Part II, s.64 prolongs the continuation of the tenancy until three months after those proceedings have been finally disposed of. There is a significant doubt over whether the tenant can at this stage give notice to terminate under s.27(2) (see Chapter 6), and so termination of the tenancy is most reliably achieved by having the proceedings finally disposed of.

Where the proceedings were issued by the tenant, it can discontinue them by serving notice, thereby terminating the tenancy three months after the date of service. If the effect is to terminate the tenancy otherwise than at the end of a rental period, there is no entitlement to apportion the rent. Discontinuance by the tenant would generally mean that it would be liable for the landlord's costs.

In the case of proceedings issued by the landlord, the tenant is not in a position to discontinue them. However, in the case of proceedings brought by the landlord under s.24(1), the tenant may instead notify the court that it does not want a new tenancy, and the court is then required to dismiss the landlord's claim, thereby bringing the tenancy to an end in accordance with s.64.

If the landlord's proceedings were brought under s.29(2), the nature of those proceedings is that the landlord is seeking to terminate the tenancy, and so the tenant may simply not oppose the claim. In that case proceedings can still be brought to a determination quite quickly, by various routes.

While the timing of the procedure may often make this impossible, if the tenant can go out of occupation of the property prior to the contractual expiry date, then the tenancy will terminate on that date by virtue of s.27(1A) (see Chapter 8). This applies regardless of whether the proceedings were issued under s.24(1) or s.29(2), or whether they were issued by tenant or landlord.

Should matters progress as far as the court ordering a new tenancy, under s.36(2) the tenant has one last chance to terminate its obligations by giving notice to revoke the order within 14 days of it having been made. This is likely to have adverse costs consequences; also the court has power to prolong the continuation of the existing tenancy significantly.

PRACTICAL SCENARIOS –THE RIGHT ANSWER FOR DIFFERENT SITUATIONS

The following scenarios do not provide a comprehensive answer to every situation which might arise in practice. That would require the anticipatory powers of a chess grandmaster. However, they do provide some practical applications of the content of the previous chapters, highlighting some of the potential complexities of the renewal procedure, in a way which it is hoped is helpful.

Scenario 1 – Court applications and competing notices

Contractual expiry date is 24 March 2021. L serves a valid *s.25* notice, indicating that the grant of a new lease will not be opposed, and terminating the lease on 28 September 2021.

It is now early September 2021. T has not yet made any court application, and no landlord's application has been served. T concludes terms for a new lease of other premises, and wishes to terminate the existing lease at the earliest possible date.

- T cannot now serve a *s.27(1)* notice, since that is only possible up to three months prior to the contractual expiry date.

- Going out of occupation now would not terminate the tenancy under *s.27(1A)*, since the contractual expiry date is past.

- T could wait until the expiry of the *s.25* notice on 28 September, and if no application is served by L, the tenancy will terminate then. However, that leaves the termination of the tenancy dependent on what action L may or may not take. It may be that L has already issued but not served a court application, in which case termination could not reliably be effected under *s.64* until three months after T had found itself in a position, L's

119

proceedings having been served, to give a notification under *s.29(5)*.

- T might issue a court application now, serve it, and immediately discontinue the action. There would be an administrative delay in issuing the proceedings, to be added to the three months after the discontinuance which would apply under *s.64*. It is possible that service of T's application would flush out a prior, unserved application by L, in which case T's application would have been invalid, and T would have to give a notification under *s.29(5)* and wait three months after that.

- The most reliable route is to serve a *s.27(2)* notice, terminating in three months' time. If it is the case that L has issued but not yet served proceedings, any *s.27(2)* notice would arguably be invalid, but T has nothing to lose by serving one anyway. Should the landlord then serve those proceedings, T could give notification under *s.29(5)*. The parties would be left to argue over whether termination had been effected by the *s.27(2)* notice or the *s.29(5)* notification, and accordingly how much further rent was to be paid, but one way or another the tenancy would have been terminated..

In the event, T serves a *s.27(2)* notice, terminating the lease on 7 December 2021. However, T also states in a covering letter that it accepts the termination date will be 28 September 2021, the date contained in the *s.25* notice. Is that correct?

Long Acre Securities Ltd v Electro Acoustic Industries Ltd [1990] 1 EGLR 91 indicates that a valid *s.27(2)* notice can be served after a valid *s.25* notice (although it should be acknowledged that there it was the *s.27(2)* notice which specified the earlier date). Assuming both notices to be valid, the earlier termination date of the two should have effect. It was therefore correct to accept that the termination date in the *s.25* would apply.

It turns out that L has not yet issued proceedings. Could L do so now, prior to 28 September 2021, and rely on *s.64* to extend the tenancy,

and therefore the rental liability, until three months after disposal of the proceedings (which might be prolonged to some extent by not serving the proceedings until required to do so by the tenant under *Civil Procedure Rules r.7.7*)?

Issue of proceedings by L subsequent to the *s.27(2)* notice would engage *s.64*, which rewrites the *s.25* notice by substituting a new termination date, i.e. the date which is three months after final determination of the renewal proceedings. Arguably, the *s.27(2)* notice remains effective despite *s.64*. It was a valid notice when served, and in the author's view there is no warrant in the wording of *s.64* for an argument that the issue of proceedings would cancel a prior valid notice. On that basis, out of the two routes to termination, once proceedings are issued it would become instead the *s.27(2)* notice which would effect termination earlier.

The landlord could potentially, therefore, extend the rental liability by issuing proceedings, though potentially only up to the *s.27(2)* date of 7 December 2021, rather than the *s.25* date of 28 September 2021.

Scenario 2 – Opposed lease renewal and discontinuance

Contractual expiry date is 28 September 2021. T serves a valid *s.26* request, seeking a new tenancy beginning on 29 September 2021. In response, L serves a counternotice indicating intention to oppose renewal. T forms the view that L will justify its ground of opposition, and in due course identifies alternative premises.

By the end of July 2021, T is negotiating a new lease of the alternative premises, but is not confident of being in occupation by 29 September. To buy time, T issues an application for a new tenancy under *s.24(1)*, but does not serve it. In the event, the new lease is executed on 24 September, for a term commencing on that date. T wishes to terminate the existing lease at the earliest possible date.

- No notice can be served under either *s.27(1)* or *s.27(2)*, because T has already served a *s.26* request (and it would be too late to serve a *s.27(1)* notice anyway).

- If T is able to go out of business occupation of the existing premises on or before the contractual expiry date, 28 September 2021, then it can rely upon *s.27(1A)*, despite having served a *s.26* request and applied to court under *s.24(1)* (*Single Horse Properties Ltd v Surrey County Council [2002] EWCA Civ 367*). The tenancy would terminate on 28 September. Needless to say, there is very little time to do this, and while T may attempt it, it would be prudent to set in train more formal means of termination as well.

- T can serve the proceedings together with a notice of discontinuance, to terminate the tenancy three months after the date the notice was given, under *s.64*.

- As in scenario 1 above, it is possible that service of T's application would flush out a prior application by L, issued before T's *s.24(1)* application, but not yet served. In that case T's application would have been invalid. T's only route to termination in that case would be to achieve final disposal of the landlord's proceedings, so that the tenancy terminates three months afterwards under *s.64*. However, unlike in scenario 1, the landlord has opposed renewal. It may therefore be assumed that its application was issued under *s.29(2)*, and so it is not possible for the tenant to give a notification under *s.29(5)*.

T may notify the landlord and the court that it does not intend to defend the claim or seek a new tenancy, and omit to file a defence. The landlord may be left to enter judgment in default, or the tenant may take the initiative by inviting the landlord to join in a consent order terminating the existing tenancy, or failing that, inviting the court to make an order for termination.

Under *s.64*, the date of termination would be three months and 21 days after the date of the judgment or court order

Scenario 3 – Long s.27(2) notice

Contractual expiry date is 28 September 2022. It is now the end of September 2021. T has identified new premises, which are still in the course of construction, and has signed an agreement for lease, conditional upon practical completion. L's construction works, plus the tenant's fit-out, are estimated to take eighteen months, so T will wish its existing tenancy to continue beyond the contractual expiry date, up to approximately the end of March 2023.

- T could simply wait to see whether L serves a *s.25* notice.

  o If no *s.25* notice is forthcoming, T will be able to serve a *s.27(2)* notice to terminate at the desired time.

  o If a *s.25* notice is eventually served specifying a termination date later than T requires, T can counter with a shorter *s.27(2)* notice, which would be effective.

  o If, however, L serves a *s.25* notice to terminate earlier than T requires, and is not amenable to agreeing an extension of time for issuing proceedings, T would need to try to manipulate the court process so as to achieve termination at the right time. This could not be guaranteed.

- T might, alternatively, take the initiative by serving a twelve-month *s.26* request. If this step could be put off until March 2022 or later, T could then simply omit to make a court application, and the tenancy would expire on the date specified in the request. However, that depends upon L not serving a *s.25* notice before March 2022, which cannot be guaranteed. Even if no such notice were served, a *s.26* request might prompt a court application by L, and if it were an application made pursuant to *s.29(2)* then achieving termination would involve some administrative delay, as discussed in Scenario 2.

  Generally, this looks like a worse option than awaiting a *s.25* notice. It might again be necessary to try to control the timetable of the court process, and moreover this would rule out the possibility of serving a *s.27(2)* notice at a later date.

- A better option may be to serve a long *s.27(2)* notice now, specifying termination in eighteen months' time, at the end of March 2022. If, for any reason L required termination earlier (perhaps an intended redevelopment project scheduled to begin in September 2022), it would probably respond by serving a *s.25* notice specifying that earlier termination date. Though there is as yet no caselaw on the point, it is thought that the shorter *s.25* notice would be valid, and effective to terminate the tenancy on the date specified in it. A landlord could not depend on that outcome, though, and would need a sufficiently strong incentive to litigate the point. The likelihood is that in most cases the landlord would see no benefit in countering the *s.27(2)* notice.

Scenario 4 – Business occupation ceases after contractual expiry date

Contractual expiry date is 24 March 2021. T remains in occupation after that date, and the tenancy continues under *s.24(1)*. L serves a *s.25* notice on 31 March 2021, specifying termination on 24 March 2022.

It is now late September 2021. T has concluded a new lease of alternative premises, and has relocated to them. It is no longer in business occupation of the original premises. T considers it is no longer obliged to pay rent to L.

- *s.27(1A)* provides, in effect, that a tenancy terminates at its contractual expiry date, if the tenant has ceased business occupation on or before that date. However, it does not apply if the business occupation ceases *after* that date, even one day after. Indeed, *s.24(3)(a)* provides that the tenancy does not come to an end after contractual expiry only by reason of ceasing to be a tenancy to which Part II of the 1954 Act applies, and equivalent provision, referring specifically to the tenant ceasing to occupy, is contained in *s.27(2)* for good measure.

- Instead, L may serve from six to three months' notice under *s.24(3)(a)* to terminate the tenancy. It is thought that this enables L to bring forward the termination to a date earlier than that specified in the *s.25* notice, for example by giving a *s.24(3)(a)* notice terminating on 7 January 2022 (although in the circumstances that may be unlikely).

- T, having realised that it must indeed pay rent to L until such time as the tenancy is effectively terminated, will not wish to wait and see whether the landlord is sufficiently obliging to serve a short *s.24(3)(a)* notice.

  o It cannot, of course, serve a *s.26* request, since a *s.25* notice has been served.

  o Neither can it serve a *s.27(1)* notice, as it is too late for that.

  o It could perhaps issue and serve an application for a new tenancy immediately, accompanied by a notice of discontinuance, thus achieving termination under *s.64* three months after the discontinuance.

It would be more straightforward to serve a *s.27(2)* notice, and *Long Acre* establishes that this can validly be done to terminate the tenancy earlier than the date specified in the landlord's *s.25* notice.

MORE BOOKS BY
LAW BRIEF PUBLISHING

A selection of our other titles available now:-

'A Practical Guide to Solicitor and Client Costs – 2nd Edition' by Robin Dunne
'Constructive Dismissal – Practice Pointers and Principles' by Benjimin Burgher
'A Practical Guide to Religion and Belief Discrimination Claims in the Workplace' by Kashif Ali
'A Practical Guide to the Law of Medical Treatment Decisions' by Ben Troke
'Fundamental Dishonesty and QOCS in Personal Injury Proceedings: Law and Practice' by Jake Rowley
'A Practical Guide to the Law in Relation to School Exclusions' by Charlotte Hadfield & Alice de Coverley
'A Practical Guide to Divorce for the Silver Separators' by Karin Walker
'The Right to be Forgotten – The Law and Practical Issues' by Melissa Stock
'A Practical Guide to Planning Law and Rights of Way in National Parks, the Broads and AONBs' by James Maurici QC, James Neill et al
'A Practical Guide to Election Law' by Tom Tabori
'A Practical Guide to the Law in Relation to Surrogacy' by Andrew Powell
'A Practical Guide to Claims Arising from Fatal Accidents – 2nd Edition' by James Patience
'A Practical Guide to the Ownership of Employee Inventions – From Entitlement to Compensation' by James Tumbridge & Ashley Roughton
'A Practical Guide to Asbestos Claims' by Jonathan Owen & Gareth McAloon
'A Practical Guide to Stamp Duty Land Tax in England and Northern Ireland' by Suzanne O'Hara
'A Practical Guide to the Law of Farming Partnerships' by Philip Whitcomb

'A Practical Guide to the Rights of Grandparents in Children Proceedings'
by Stuart Barlow

'NHS Whistleblowing and the Law' by Joseph England

'Employment Law and the Gig Economy' by Nigel Mackay & Annie Powell

'A Practical Guide to Noise Induced Hearing Loss (NIHL) Claims'
by Andrew Mckie, Ian Skeate, Gareth McAloon

'An Introduction to Beauty Negligence Claims – A Practical Guide for the Personal
Injury Practitioner' by Greg Almond

'Intercompany Agreements for Transfer Pricing Compliance' by Paul Sutton

'Zen and the Art of Mediation' by Martin Plowman

'A Practical Guide to the SRA Principles, Individual and Law Firm Codes of
Conduct 2019 – What Every Law Firm Needs to Know' by Paul Bennett

'A Practical Guide to Adoption for Family Lawyers' by Graham Pegg

'A Practical Guide to Industrial Disease Claims' by Andrew Mckie & Ian Skeate

'A Practical Guide to Redundancy' by Philip Hyland

'A Practical Guide to Vicarious Liability' by Mariel Irvine

'A Practical Guide to Applications for Landlord's Consent and Variation of Leases'
by Mark Shelton

'A Practical Guide to Relief from Sanctions Post-Mitchell and Denton'
by Peter Causton

'A Practical Guide to Equity Release for Advisors' by Paul Sams

'A Practical Guide to the Law Relating to Food' by Ian Thomas

'A Practical Guide to Financial Services Claims' by Chris Hegarty

'The Law of Houses in Multiple Occupation: A Practical Guide to HMO
Proceedings' by Julian Hunt

'A Practical Guide to Unlawful Eviction and Harassment' by Stephanie Lovegrove

'Occupiers, Highways and Defective Premises Claims: A Practical Guide Post-
Jackson – 2nd Edition' by Andrew Mckie

'A Practical Guide to Financial Ombudsman Service Claims' by Adam Temple & Robert Scrivenor
'A Practical Guide to Advising Schools on Employment Law' by Jonathan Holden
'A Practical Guide to Running Housing Disrepair and Cavity Wall Claims: 2nd Edition' by Andrew Mckie & Ian Skeate
'A Practical Guide to Holiday Sickness Claims – 2nd Edition' by Andrew Mckie & Ian Skeate
'Arguments and Tactics for Personal Injury and Clinical Negligence Claims' by Dorian Williams
'A Practical Guide to Drone Law' by Rufus Ballaster, Andrew Firman, Eleanor Clot
'A Practical Guide to Compliance for Personal Injury Firms Working With Claims Management Companies' by Paul Bennett
'A Practical Guide to Dog Law for Owners and Others' by Andrea Pitt
'RTA Allegations of Fraud in a Post-Jackson Era: The Handbook – 2nd Edition' by Andrew Mckie
'RTA Personal Injury Claims: A Practical Guide Post-Jackson' by Andrew Mckie
'On Experts: CPR35 for Lawyers and Experts' by David Boyle
'An Introduction to Personal Injury Law' by David Boyle
'A Practical Guide to Subtle Brain Injury Claims' by Pankaj Madan

These books and more are available to order online direct from the publisher at www.lawbriefpublishing.com, where you can also read free sample chapters. For any queries, contact us on 0844 587 2383 or mail@lawbriefpublishing.com.

Our books are also usually in stock at www.amazon.co.uk with free next day delivery for Prime members, and at good legal bookshops such as Wildy & Sons.

We are regularly launching new books in our series of practical day-to-day practitioners' guides. Visit our website and join our free newsletter to be kept informed and to receive special offers, free chapters, etc.

You can also follow us on Twitter at www.twitter.com/lawbriefpub.

Lightning Source UK Ltd.
Milton Keynes UK
UKHW011002251121
394533UK00004B/152